BY SOME MIRACLE
I MADE IT OUT OF THERE

BY SOME MIRACLE I MADE IT OUT OF THERE

A Memoir

TOM SIZEMORE WITH ANNA DAVID

ATRIA PAPERBACK

New York • London • Toronto • Sydney • New Delhi

 **ATRIA** PAPERBACK
An Imprint of Simon & Schuster, Inc.
1230 Avenue of the Americas
New York, NY 10020

First Atria Paperback edition March 2016

ATRIA PAPERBACK and colophon are trademarks of Simon & Schuster, Inc.

For information about special discounts for bulk purchases, please contact
Simon & Schuster Special Sales at 1-866-506-1949 or business@simonandschuster.com.

The Simon & Schuster Speakers Bureau can bring authors to your live event. For more
information or to book an event, contact the Simon & Schuster Speakers Bureau at
1-866-248-3049 or visit our website at www.simonspeakers.com.

Designed by Dana Sloan

Manufactured in the United States of America

10 9 8 7 6 5 4 3 2 1

Library of Congress Cataloging-in-Publication Data

Sizemore, Tom, 1961–
    By some miracle I made it out of there : a memoir / by Tom Sizemore with Anna David. —
First Atria Books hardcover edition.
        pages cm
    1. Sizemore, Tom, 1961– 2. Actors—United States—Biography. 3. Methamphetamine
abuse—California—Biography. 4. Drug addicts—Rehabilitation—California—Biography. I.
David, Anna, 1970– II. Title.
    PN2287.S393A3 2013
    791.4302'8092—dc23
    [B]

                                                    2012048280

ISBN 978-1-4516-8167-3
ISBN 978-1-4516-8168-0 (pbk)
ISBN 978-1-4516-8169-7 (ebook)

For my two sons, Jayden and Jagger;
my mother, Judy Sizemore;
Monroe Allen; and Anna David

"What if by some miracle we stay, then actually make it out of here?"

—Sergeant Mike Horvath (Tom Sizemore), *Saving Private Ryan*

PREFACE

I NEVER EXPECTED TO be more infamous than famous. Before my arrest in 2003, the only things that the public knew about me were from my work. You knew about *Heat* and *Natural Born Killers* and *Saving Private Ryan*. The interviews I gave were, if not boring, then at least completely benign. Back when we were promoting *Natural Born Killers* and I was dating Juliette Lewis, if a reporter said, "So tell me about Juliette Lewis," I'd know what they were getting at—the fact that we were having an affair—but I would play completely dumb. I'd say, "You saw that movie, and you saw her play Mallory Knox, and if you want to know anything else about her, I'd say you just have to watch the movie again."

They'd say, "What do you mean?" and I'd say something like "She's just a wild child." Something dumb, and it would get picked up. That's actually one of the quotes I'm known for on Juliette: "She's a wild child." One of the stupidest things I've ever said.

Still, because I said nothing, all you knew about me was the work. But then everything fell apart and there was a descent into complete fucking weirdness and non sequiturs. I went on *A Current Affair* in 2005 and talked about how I once couldn't find my way home. I was making a joke and it was reported as serious news—"Actor Tom Sizemore Can't Find His Way Home"—but my point is that I was supposed to be on television talking about being an actor. I think it's safe to say that things are out of control when headlines are stating that you can't find your way home.

And here's how I feel at this point: I'd never hire me. If I weren't me, I wouldn't hire Tom Sizemore to make coffee or throw confetti on himself. I'd think, "This guy went to prison. Are you kidding? He used a Whizzinator! I don't want him in my building! You think I want him on my show?" I wouldn't have given myself the chances other people have been generous enough to give me.

I've led an interesting life, but I can't tell you what I'd give to be the guy you didn't know anything about. What I'd give to be someone like Tom Hanks, where, when you thought of me, you'd say, "Oh, Tom—he's really something else, huh? America's favorite neighbor. America's favorite son."

Of course, that's not me. I've done a lot of things that would make that impossible, and I know that telling you all about them probably won't help me to become America's favorite son. But it may help you to understand how everything happened the way it did and a bit more about what was going on behind those ugly headlines. For now, I've come out on the other side—found a way to get off drugs and build a career that I'm proud of again—but I also know that, as a sober addict, all I really have is today. And for that, I'm incredibly grateful.

I'm also grateful that you still care about me. Without that, I'd never have made it this far.

Tom Sizemore
August 2012

BY SOME MIRACLE
I MADE IT OUT OF THERE

CRYSTAL

REALLY, ALL I knew about crystal meth before I did it was that it was supposed to be an aphrodisiac of sorts: it apparently transformed men into Superman in bed. And look, you read "Makes your penis incredibly hard and Superman-like" and it's going to get filed away in your mind, even if you're sober—as I was in 2001.

By then, my former heroin addiction and the rehabs I'd been to felt like they were pretty far back in the past. And the truth of the matter is that I didn't really want to be sober.

That's part of why I don't blame Heidi Fleiss for what happened. But before I get into that, let's get one thing straight: I didn't expect to fall for her. Still, I was hooked on sex with her from the beginning: Heidi had a quality that I've never been able to pinpoint exactly, but she had the ability to make any shameful associations with sex disappear.

One of the first nights she came over to my house, she laid out a little bit of meth on the dresser in my bedroom. I had been lying on the bed with my back turned, but I heard what she was doing.

"That's coke, right?" I asked. Even though she knew I'd been in trouble with heroin years before, I hadn't made a big deal about how I hadn't been doing drugs. I really didn't talk about it at all.

"Nope," she said. "It's trailer park dope."

That's when I got up and started walking around the bed. She wasn't trying to get me to do it; she was just doing her thing. But I watched her do her thing with interest.

"So that's that meth shit?" I asked. Keep in mind that this was in 2001; there wasn't a lot out there about meth yet. "That crystal shit?"

She nodded, and that was all it took. I grabbed the straw from her.

"Be careful—it's strong," she said.

I was trying to be cool, so I said something like "I know how to do dope, bitch." And then I did a line.

Ten seconds later, I was flying—fucking flying. I hadn't done coke in years, but this was nothing like coke. It was the most intense thing I'd ever felt. I was instantly more energetic and euphoric than I'd ever been—it was like hurling forward at the speed of light—and I knew, even though I couldn't admit it at the time, that human beings simply weren't meant to feel *that* good. I turned around and said, "What the fuck, are you trying to kill me?"

She didn't answer because she was already taking off her clothes. And that's when I discovered that everything I'd read about the Superman powers was true. At that moment, I wanted to fuck her more than I wanted to breathe.

Later, Heidi told me she'd never seen meth impact anyone the way it did me—sexually, that is. On meth, I could orgasm and never lose my erection. I'd come four or five times, and each one would be better—more intense—than the last. I was already rapacious before meth, but meth made me sexualize everything and everyone. I started to associate the drug and sex right away, whereas it generally takes other people some time before that occurs.

Heidi had already been doing meth for a while by then. She was actually at the point where she was dreading having to do it and was ready to stop. But I was just getting going. I didn't know how dangerous it was—it's not like it came with some skull and crossbones on it—and people just didn't know then. I thought I was doing something that was just going to lead to more fun and bring more pleasure to my life. I didn't understand then, or in any way anticipate, that I'd soon have to do it to handle my every mood and feeling.

I woke up the next morning and didn't even think about it. Heidi went home, and I got up and worked out. If only I'd known then what getting involved with Heidi, and with meth, would do to me. I had no idea that my life would never be the same.

CHAPTER 1

DETROIT

THE PART OF Detroit I was born in—Corktown—wasn't exactly Beverly Hills. It was a small enclave of poor, working-class white people located near Tiger Stadium, a stadium that's since been torn down but used to be where the Detroit Tigers would play. Although my family's financial situation changed later, when my dad became a lawyer, we didn't have a lot in the beginning. It was a very blue-collar, lower-middle-class upbringing.

My dad—Thomas Edward Sizemore Sr.—was one of the more handsome men you might ever see, and he's always been very intelligent. Though he came from southern migrant farmers, previous generations of Sizemores were more prominent citizens. If you go to Clay County, Kentucky, where most of them are from, you'll see in the halls of the county buildings pictures, plaques of Sizemore men who were sheriffs, teachers, tax assessors, and collectors. Public minutes and records also show that Sizemore men were involved in the planning, construction, and maintenance of the roads there. Essentially, if you show up just about anywhere in Clay County and mention the family name Sizemore, you'll probably discover that the person you're talking to is related, married to, or knows a Sizemore. There's even an old Kentucky saying: "Where there's dirt, you'll find a Sizemore."

A long-standing Sizemore tradition—and one that I carried out myself—was to pull up stakes and move to a distant place in order to improve the lot you've been given in life and change the direction and future of the family. And my father's father, Blevins Sizemore, did just that when he moved from Clay County to Detroit, Michigan, in the early 1940s with my grandmother Vina and their children—my father and his siblings Carl, Sally, Ernie, Keith, and Patsy. The children were born in that order except that my father was born after Carl. They also had another brother, Donald Edward, my grandparents' firstborn, but he died when he was a year old. My grandmother always carried a picture of him in her wallet, and I used to look at it sometimes when visiting with her. I don't think my grandparents ever fully got over his death, and it probably influenced to a large degree the permissiveness of the way they parented. For sure, the boys could almost do no wrong, however shocking their behavior might be to others. Carl and Keith both became full-blown heroin addicts, and Carl was dealing heroin out of the house to support his and Keith's habit. They were also both thieves and fences. Ernie was smoking pot and dropping LSD, and Grandpa Sizemore always made sure they all had cigarettes.

Even though it was wartime my grandfather Blevins couldn't serve because he was blind in one eye. He'd actually been kicked out of school in fourth grade because the teachers back then thought his eye problem might have been contagious. Apparently, though, he simply had really bad cataracts in both eyes, though one eye was worse than the other.

Despite his vision problems, Blevins started working for Micromatic Hone Corporation, a machinist shop, where he honed and shaped steel. The family was dirt poor. They had just two chairs at the table for the two adults to sit in (the children stood to eat) and no phone. And Blevins was a really bad alcoholic. If Vina didn't get ahold of Blevins's paycheck before he did, he would be down at the bar, having spent the whole thing on booze and pissed himself. Vina was always sending Sally down to the bar to bring her drunken dad home.

I remember as a kid seeing Uncle Carl get up from where we were all playing cards and go out to the entry vestibule, where he would make his drug deals. It was my first exposure to drugs and the way they had to be kept secret. Every half hour or so there'd be someone knocking at the door. Carl would let that person into the vestibule, which was closed off from the living room, find out what they wanted, then go into the basement where he kept the heroin, get the requested amount, return to the vestibule, and make the deal. When I asked my aunt Sally what was going on, she said, "Your uncle's selling drugs." I remember saying to her, "That's what I thought! Is it dangerous?" She said, "Oh no. Not at all, Tommy. He's a good drug dealer." I think I was nine when that conversation took place.

But the truth is that I really liked Uncle Carl and Uncle Keith. Carl was a kind of bebop jazz aficionado and Keith was something of a hippie who loved the Rolling Stones. I remember one year when Keith returned home for Christmas. I was about twelve and asked him what he'd been reading. He said, "Tom, this drug problem has gotten out of control and I just decided to read the dictionary—I figured all the books were in it." They were both characters.

Somehow, even though he was in that environment, my father never did drugs, and he was the only one out of all his siblings to graduate from high school. I know that he once took a hit off a joint that his brother Ernie suggested he try and he later told me that it felt like the floor opened up and every monster and insecurity in his life came out and laughed at him. He never did a mind-altering drug again. He used to say that his addiction was reading. In retrospect, he really picked an addiction that fit his very private, almost shut-away, personality. You could talk to this fool for a half hour while he read, and if you asked him what was for dinner, he'd say, "Food." You'd ask what kind and he'd say, "Ask your mother." You'd ask where she was and he'd say, "Thomas, can't you tell that I'm reading?" That was actually kind of a funny routine we had.

My mom's family came to Detroit under circumstances not unlike the Sizemores', and there was a bit of mystery around my grandfather Sam Schannault's racial heritage. He always thought of himself as a white man, but he was the product of a union between an American Indian sharecropper named Nina and a Georgia plantation owner of French ancestry named Mr. Chennault; I believe my grandfather later changed the spelling to Schannault. Mr. Chennault was married and had a bunch of children who lived in the plantation's main estate—a very large, luxurious home that I think is now an historical site in Georgia. When Mr. Chennault died, Nina and her kids, including my grandfather, who was maybe four years old, were expelled from the plantation.

When he grew up, my grandfather Schannault worked three jobs to keep his family off welfare. He'd do the morning shift in one factory and the evening shift at another, and also worked at a gas station. He also made their house into an after-hours joint in order to make extra money. You couldn't buy liquor after 2 A.M., so Sam would open up his doors and sell it, running what is called a blind pig. Everyone in town who liked to drink—including, on occasion, Blevins Sizemore—would show up there. Sam wasn't an alcoholic but he and my grandma Schannault both drank. They really only had the club to make extra money. As a little girl, my mom hated all the people traipsing through the house late at night, talking loudly and laughing as drunks do, making the place stink of beer and cigarettes.

Sam didn't age all that well: welding in the factory eventually gave him multiple hernias and made one of his arms significantly longer than the other. I also believe he slept about three hours a night because he worked roughly twenty-one hours a day. Still, he was the toughest man I ever met in my life. As a teenager he was about five foot nine but all brawny steel, and he and his brother Frank would go to bars in Tipton, Georgia, where they'd bet everyone there that Sam could beat anyone in a fight. And that's exactly what he'd do—beat everyone. I hear his record was 119-0. My great-uncle Frank would supposedly say, "Sam, I'm afraid you're going to end up killing one of these men one day."

My mom was the fifth of Sam and Mildred Schannault's kids. The order went Barbara, Shirley, Ronnie, Jerome, my mom, Larry, and Barry. Ronnie was friends with my dad, whom he very affectionately called "Big Ed," and the two family houses were just a few streets away from each other. Later, Ronnie realized he was gay and ran away to New York. It was a different time, and I think he was sort of hiding out in shame. My mom was really the only one in the family who stayed in touch with him and he didn't come home again until years later—the early 1980s—when he had AIDS and was dying.

Jerome ended up becoming a big pimp in Detroit. He had these two massage parlors that were really whorehouses called Foxy Ladies and Gentleman's Retreat and everyone in Detroit (including the *Detroit News* and *Detroit Free Press*) called Jerome the Fat Man or the Slob because, honestly, he was kind of overweight and generally didn't dress well. He was a total character. He'd say things like "Here I am providing a social service—do you think most of the slobs walking through my door could get that kind of pussy on their own?—and those corrupt, no-good rats want to incarcerate me. For sellin' honey? Doesn't it make you sick? Disgusting. It's disgusting." He'd go off on these rants about how "the most twisted" whorehouses in the world were in Washington, D.C. (and he knew firsthand, since he'd been to them all!) and here the authorities were bothering him.

My mom, Judith Kay Schannault, met my dad when she was thirteen and he was fourteen. Apparently they even had some sort of "faux marriage" back when they were kids. My mom was incredibly beautiful and had a lot of boys wooing her.

Like I said, my dad was incredibly smart: it literally said "Boy Genius" beneath his high school senior yearbook picture. And one day when he was nine years old, his teacher brought him home from school so he could talk to his parents. The teacher said to Blevins, "Your son's too smart to be in this school—he needs to go to a smart kids' school." Blevins was drunk at the time and couldn't really hear what the teacher was saying, so he pulled out a shotgun and told the teacher to get off his porch. And then, because Blevins was so much to deal with, my grandmother didn't want to confront him and upset him further, so my dad never did end up switching schools.

And yet even though he came from those circumstances, he ended up getting a full scholarship to Harvard. He went there for his freshman year and cleaned dorms to make pocket money. But he felt entirely out of place in his Salvation Army clothes. He came from a family of hillbillies who lived on a dirt floor, and all the Harvard kids were from another world. And even though he was getting straight As, he could never adjust to the Harvard environment. So one Friday he left his last class, walked to the bus station, and took the bus to New York's Pennsylvania Station. He was thinking about becoming a writer—he was artistic and well-read—or joining the Foreign Legion, but after about a day walking around more or less aimlessly, he realized he had just enough money to take a bus home to Detroit.

My guess is that my dad really missed my mom when he was at Harvard, and she was one of the reasons he wanted to come home. So he did. Harvard called Detroit—they had to call a neighbor because my dad's family didn't have a phone—and they told him he could come back, that everything was fine. They knew that he was gifted, and they understood his circumstances, but I think he was just too ashamed to go back. So he never returned to Harvard, and that's something he has always regretted. Still, the life my dad was able to build with my mom was definitely an improvement over his childhood; my dad really got his family out of the Dark Ages.

My parents got married in a simple ceremony in Belle Isle Park in Detroit when my mom was nineteen. I was born in 1961, and I guess the place my parents were living in at that point was pretty bad. It didn't even have any heat. My dad called the landlord to try to get the heat turned on there and was told, "What are you talking about? There's no heat there to turn on." Then one day the toilet fell through the floor because the floors were about as thin as sandpaper. My mom said, "I'm not staying here with my baby—I'm freezing to death, the toilet just fell through the floor, and I've had enough." So when I was just a few weeks old we moved into a two-family flat on the predominantly white, working-class east side of Detroit with my maternal grandparents. We lived upstairs and they took the downstairs flat.

My brother Aaron was born two years later and we lived in the two-family flat for about eleven years. Our family actually still owns it, and my mom's younger brother Barry lives there now. Because my parents both worked when Aaron and I were little—my mom for the ombudsman's office and my dad teaching mentally challenged kids—

my grandmother looked after us a lot. She was really nurturing and, in a lot of ways, I felt like I had two moms. I got a lot of attention early on: I was a good boy, quite curious, and I was also the first grandchild of both my parents' parents. And I was smart. I talked and learned to read early—I was supposedly saying complete sentences by the time Aaron was born and was reading by the age of four.

We didn't really have a car because we kept thinking we were getting deals, only to learn we'd actually been screwed over. I remember my dad at one point got a Jaguar for two hundred bucks when at the time they cost $75,000. Mom said to him, "If you bought the car for two hundred dollars, it stands to reason that it's not any good. There's got to be something wrong with it." My uncle Jerome opened the hood—my dad had never even opened it to look—and there was no engine. Jerome said, "Ain't got no engine, first thing, that's not good." My dad just wasn't good with stuff like that.

When I was in second grade and Aaron was in kindergarten, we moved to Ames, Iowa, for a year because my dad got a job teaching philosophy at Iowa State University. We were just a few weeks into living there when my parents decided one day, in the dead of an Iowa winter, to drop me and Aaron off to see the play *Rumpelstiltskin*. We'd never been to a play before, and it really wasn't our kind of thing, but my parents must have had something they wanted to do that day because they didn't tend to ever leave us anywhere on our own. But that day they took us to this theater, dropped us off, and told us to watch the play and then wait for them to come pick us up when it was over.

Aaron and I started watching the play and it was the most boring thing I'd ever seen in my life. It's ironic that my first experience with theater was so terrible, given that I later came to love it so much, but what can I say? I still don't like bad theater and this was bad. When the actors came out and started yelling, "Hark!" I turned to Aaron and said, "They've got to be kidding."

After about five minutes, I told Aaron we should leave and he said that we couldn't—that we'd promised Mom and Dad we'd stay until the end and wait for them to come pick us up. I was frustrated but agreed to stay, and then counted the minutes until the curtain went down an hour and ten minutes later. We went out into the lobby, and that's when we found out that it wasn't over—that it was only the intermission and we had two more acts to go. Now it was a brisk winter day, maybe twenty degrees, with tons of snow piled on the sides of the streets, some of it higher than our shoulders. We'd just moved to the area and I didn't know the first thing about the neighborhood or town we were in but I didn't care; I'd had it. I turned to Aaron and said, "I'm going home, you want to come with me?" Honestly, I hated that play so much that I wouldn't have cared if I had to walk to the center of the earth.

Aaron looked at me like I was crazy. "We're miles from home!" he said with these big, wide eyes. I told him I knew that but that I could figure out the way back. He was torn. I could tell he was terrified to go with me but he knew I was serious, and he was also scared to stay at the play by himself. And the thing is, he had every reason to be scared. I didn't know my way home at all and was completely bluffing.

Still, I had this vague idea that if we made a right, then a left, then another quick right, it would put us in the direction of where we lived. The snow was up to our hips, but I ignored that. "Come on!" I said to Aaron and just started walking the way I thought was right. He followed me but he was still panicked—he was saying things like "We're gonna die, we should go back. We're little." And I told him, "I don't care—I'd rather die than watch any more of that play." At the time, I felt like I meant it. He kept asking me if I was sure I knew where I was going, and the truth was, the more we walked, the less certain I was.

But I saw how worried he looked and I remember saying to myself, "He can't handle the truth." So I told him yes, of course I was sure.

It turned out that I did. Or I got lucky. All I know is that we walked a long time in the freezing snow and eventually wound up at home. Even though we were both frozen solid, I kept telling Aaron that I wasn't cold at all. That was probably my first acting job: convincing my little brother that I was almost warm in temperatures so cold. By the last two blocks I actually had to hold him to keep him from freezing, but I was still telling him it wasn't cold out. Then, when we got to our front door and saw our dad coming down the steps, I told Aaron to act normal and not say a word. I said, "Hey, Dad, John's mother drove us home, the play just ended."

At first he believed us but then he felt our faces, which were frozen. He asked, "What's wrong with your faces? Why are they so red and so cold?" I said, "Nothing, something must be wrong with your hands." I thought that was pretty clever. He said, "There's nothing wrong with my hands." I said, "How do you know, are you a doctor?" Then he said, "Thomas, sit down." I could tell he knew what had happened, and I thought I was going to get in trouble for putting my brother at risk. But instead he said he was really proud of me. He said to Aaron, "You're lucky you've got Tom." And that's why that day sticks out so much in my head. My dad wasn't easy to impress, but me being able to find our way home from miles away when we'd just moved in really impressed him.

But even though I was a tough little kid who could usually act strong in front of my brother, when I went to bed at night I always thought that someone was going to break into our house. I shared a bedroom with Aaron, and I'd always ask him if he heard certain noises I was sure I heard. Sometimes I'd even be crying when I asked. Then I'd beg Aaron not to fall asleep until I had. He'd try his best. When I was really scared, I'd go in and sleep with my parents.

I really wanted to be strong and smart like my father, who, after teaching for a long time, decided he wanted to be a lawyer, so he enrolled in law school at the University of Michigan. He never went to a class—he just read the books and took the tests because we were living in Detroit and he didn't want to have to drive to Ann Arbor—but he was getting straight A's. One day in the middle of his second year there, when he went in to get his test score, his instructor said, "You live!" My dad said, "Sorry I haven't been here. I have children to take care of." The instructor asked him if he could stay after class to talk and my dad said, "I really can't. It's just the law; what do you want to talk about?"

When he graduated, he practiced corporate law at one of the most respected firms in the nation, where the thinking was basically, if you have a problem and you can't solve it, take it to Sizemore.

But because my dad had never gotten anything but A's, satisfying him was next to impossible. I was in honors algebra as an eighth grader and I should have been in regular algebra, but the thinking was that because my father would have been in honors algebra, so should I. But I knew I was screwed in that class. It was like joining the track team and having to run at five in the morning. I just knew I wasn't going to be able do it right. I was not as high an achiever as he was, so I fell behind, and once you fall behind in math, you're screwed. And he wouldn't let me move to regular algebra. If you had put me in that class and spun me around with my eyes closed, I wouldn't know where I sat; that's how confused I was.

I'd get really scared—probably irrationally scared—whenever my father tutored me. He was a tough guy, and when I was slow to understand some of the algebra problems, he'd get frustrated with me. He was just trying to push me to do better, and his manner was a little gruff. At one point my mom saw the way he was talking to me during one of these tutoring sessions and she said, "Edward, that's enough!" He ignored her and she said again, "I said that's enough! That is my son, too, and that is enough!" he finally looked up. She said, "How do you expect anybody to even be able to read the word *the* when you're in his ear like that? The pressure you're applying right now is just wrong. I want you to leave this room." I'd never seen my mom really get that hard with him. And because of that, he knew he was wrong. He started to say something, but she went, "Stop it. Leave him alone and get away from him. You're scaring him."

Another bad incident with my dad happened when I was in fifth grade and the music teacher picked me to sing "Silent Night" at the Christmas concert. It was a big deal because that role had always gone to a sixth grader and a girl, so I was really excited. But the night of the performance, I didn't want my hair the way my dad wanted it, and I didn't want to wear what he wanted me to wear. We had an argument about it—which he won and made me dissolve into tears. The fight escalated, and I ended up weeping: pictures from that day show how distraught I was.

When we got to school for the concert, my friends could tell I'd been crying. One of them, Michael, took me into a classroom and said, "Hey, Tom, are you okay?" He was so sweet. I told him what had happened and he said, "Forget about your dad; he can't even do birthday parties." I guess my dad had screwed up the game of Pin the Tail on the Donkey at Aaron's recent birthday party. Then Michael went and got this girl Agnes, who was sort of my girlfriend. She came back to talk to me, and I remember her looking like a concerned Meryl Streep. She said, "Tom, your father's a mean person sometimes, but he loves you."

I said, "What about my hair?" She said, "It looks great," though she told me later it actually looked like shit: all the curls had been combed out of it, and I looked like I had a Bobby Sherman haircut. And I had on this dumb electric-blue shirt—I'd never worn electric blue in my fucking life—and I was so uncomfortable. I said, "What about this shirt?" and she said, "It's beautiful." She told me later she thought it was a terrible shirt, but she went into the hall and told this other little girl, "Go in there and tell him his hair and shirt look nice, because they're awful." Those were my core friends, and we took care of each other: we knew each other's parents, and we were helping each other become little people.

Thanks to Michael and Agnes, I started to feel much better and when I went up to sing the song, the singing teacher, Miss Stohl, looked at me and said, "You can do this, honey." I remember her playing the chord on the piano and then saying, "It's Christmas." Thinking about that moment makes me want to cry because she was so goddamn sweet. She looked at me through the whole song and mouthed the words to me until she knew I could handle it on my own.

When I hit the high notes, I saw a few people out there with tears in their eyes, including my mom and Miss Stohl, and when I finished, I felt like I was a star. There were about two hundred people there, and I literally had a receiving line afterward. It was such a precursor of what was to come: on the one hand, I loved the adulation, but at the same time I felt uncomfortable.

To discover that I could be as upset as I was and still come through made me feel like I could survive anything. And I think that's probably when I realized I was a performer.

THINGS ARE DIFFERENT now, but when I was a kid your parents could whip your ass in the front yard and no one would look twice. My mom would say, "Be home by seven thirty," and if you weren't home at seven thirty, you got your ass kicked. And it worked: I was usually home at seven thirty. I don't think there's anything wrong with that: it gets your point across.

At the same time that our parents were tough with us, Aaron and I both truly idolized our father. To us, he was like a Kennedy. I remember when Bobby Kennedy came to Detroit while he was running for president in 1968. I was seven years old. In the predawn hours my dad put me on his shoulders and we went out to Hart Plaza, where RFK was going to appear at noon, and started waiting for him. It was about five in the morning. When hours later Kennedy came out— with this beautiful tan, wearing a white shirt with his sleeves rolled up and with the sun hitting his hair in a way that made it look like pure spun gold—I just loved him. And the way he smiled and the way he talked only made me love him more. I remember thinking, "My dad's like him."

On his best days, my dad was the greatest father who ever lived: he learned everything he could about baseball so he could talk to us about it and take us to ball games. He hugged us and told us he loved us and how happy he was that we were his children. He'd play Beatles songs for us and write down the lyrics so we could learn them. He taught us to play pinochle and hearts; he even tried to teach us bridge. When we were little, he read to us every night, and then, when we got older, he made us summer reading lists that included books like *The Catcher in the Rye* and *A Separate Peace*. But probably the most important thing he did was explain to us that everyone was created equal. Because of where we were living and the way people thought back then, we had plenty of people around us who were racist and homophobic and sexist. And he'd explain to us that being that way wasn't right. And I just thought he was so smart. Mom wanted us to go to church, and he would say things like "Judy, how can you believe in this shit? Supposedly God's got these Ten Commandments and if you fuck those up, you get eternal damnation, but at the same time He always loves you? How does that work? And how come He doesn't pay income taxes? I'm telling you, this whole thing's a racket!" He'd say things like "There's a whole world out there, Tommy." He's the one who turned me on to Chet Baker and Marlon Brando and really pushed me to succeed.

Still, it was very much a mixed bag: the good parenting was very good and the bad parenting was often abysmal, and very hurtful. And that was ultimately more important than the good parenting because it left some very bad psychic scars.

My brother Aaron and my dad had a complicated relationship. Aaron, like my dad, is brilliant: he can play the guitar very well, even though he's never had a lesson; he was the best track runner and football player and also a straight-A student. My brother was my best friend when we were little. I remember when I was seven and Aaron was five and an older boy threw a baseball at him very hard. I said to the kid who did it, "What are you doing? He's a kid." The boy said something like "It'll teach 'em." And then I hit this fucker in the face. I didn't want anyone messing with my brother. For a long time Aaron was that typical younger brother, and I felt like I couldn't shake him, but after a while, I didn't want to shake him anymore. He was a sweet kid. And later he not only caught up to me physically, but started doing push-ups and became much tougher.

I don't think all of the other ways we were living were healthy. It was really important to my parents that we excelled in school—it was always "We want you to go to Harvard like your father did. You can't get B's, you have to get A's." But I don't think it's right to think that you have to get an A and you have to win the football game or else you're a fucking asshole. Yet that's how I was brought up and, when you're twelve years old, that's not a way to be talked to. I didn't want to be called those names, so I became obsessively ambitious. I decided I was going to do everything I could to be the best student and athlete I could, and I missed out on a lot of things in my youth as a result. I saw life in really black-and-white terms: either you win or you're a piece of shit. When I became an actor, I had the exact same mentality.

When I was in eighth grade, we moved north to Shelby Township, near Utica, Michigan; it was a beautiful time in our lives in many ways. I was on the honor roll and was quarterback on the football team. Playing football meant a lot to me, and I took a lot of pride in my athletic accomplishments in general. I'd played in a summer basketball program in Detroit, where I'd been the only white kid to make the squad, but being quarterback was even better.

However, things took a dramatic shift when I was in tenth grade and my dad met another woman. Suzanne had come to him for legal help after her husband was killed in a motorcycle accident; one thing led to another, and my dad and Suzanne ended up falling for each other.

All I knew at the time was that the man the town considered like Abe Lincoln—the bearded, brilliant attorney—suddenly fell off his pedestal. The realization about what was going on was slow. It all started when my best friend in Utica, a kid named Brian Hagel, who was nearly ubiquitous in my home at the time, said something one night when he was visiting. Brian's parents had gotten divorced after his dad had an affair, and one night when my dad was "working late" again for the umpteenth time in recent weeks, Brian asked where my dad was. I said, "He's working late." And he just immediately busted out with "Your dad's got a girlfriend." Aaron and I were both sure that Brian was wrong. Something like that just didn't seem possible.

I don't know how long it was afterward that my mom found out. I think she started getting suspicious, too, or maybe she heard Brian say that. So one night when my dad was supposedly working late, she called his firm and asked where he was. The security guard there wasn't supposed to tell you if someone had signed in or out, but she was able to get the guard to go up and check Dad's office. The guard reported back that he wasn't there.

When my dad got home that night, we were already asleep— Aaron and I had fallen asleep in the living room on the pullout couch and our little brother Paul, who was a newborn, was asleep in his bedroom. My mom accused my dad of having an affair, I guess, and I just remember waking up to screaming. It turned into this really big, disturbing evening where a lot of ugly things were said and Paulie was crying. The family was never the same after that. I was never the same.

I was, quite honestly, traumatized. It was like all the denial suddenly ripped away and I saw that my dad wasn't perfect—he wasn't the greatest man who had ever lived. It was an ugly divorce, too: it lasted from when I was fifteen until I was eighteen. We had been a very close family who did everything together, and this new state of affairs was a real shock. Neither of my parents handled the situation particularly well. Dad was going back and forth between our home and Suzanne's for a long time; he'd swear things were over with her and then suddenly he just wouldn't come home. And it would break our hearts.

One time he drove up in Suzanne's Ford Pinto, and I was so pissed-off that I took a brick and tossed it right at the window, shattering the glass. But I wasn't the only one who was angry: my mom was livid. One time she drove over to Suzanne's and pulled a tablecloth off the table, sending all the plants and everything else on it flying. Suzanne was hiding upstairs in a linen closet the whole time. My mom found her up there and told her off. It was ugly, although I understood my mother's rage.

Another day, my dad was carrying the TV out of the house while he and my mom were fighting, and they got so angry at each other he chucked the TV right through the kitchen window. The next day, my mom went down to the TV store and said, "My husband likes to throw TVs through the window." The guy at the store said, "He should get another hobby." But I guess he felt bad for her because he gave her a free TV.

Our neighbor, a very sweet lady named Fern, was always counseling my mom about the situation—telling her that she had to save her marriage and saying that my dad was just going through a midlife crisis and would never stay with Suzanne. Fern would tell my mom to never leave her marital home and never let another woman get her husband. My mom tried so hard to make it work, but at a certain point, she just got fed up. The summer between my tenth- and eleventh-grade years, she packed us up and we returned to Detroit, where we moved back in with Grandma and Grandpa. We didn't see my dad that entire summer, but my mom and dad decided to reunite that fall, so we went back to the house in Utica. It wasn't long before the same pattern began to emerge: Dad would start staying at Suzanne's and not coming home.

After a little while my mom couldn't deal with my dad's back-and-forth anymore, so we moved out of the house again after the school year. This was a real separation—not like the one that we'd just had for the summer. We rented a U-Haul, which Aaron, two of my friends from Shelby Township, and I loaded up with all of our furniture and clothes. I don't remember this, but my mom has told me that my dad was lying on the couch, quietly crying the whole time we were packing and leaving. She and Aaron drove the U-Haul back to Detroit while I took a separate car there with my friends. Aaron told me afterward that my mom was really worried the whole drive; he kept telling her everything would be okay and she just continued smoking cigarettes and looking concerned, asking him if he really thought so.

As I said, things really changed for me while all of this drama was going on with my parents. I was just so angry with my father, and I couldn't seem to let go of it. I had been such a good student at a very demanding school and excelling at both basketball and football, but so much of that was to please my dad that I felt conflicted about continuing to try so hard.

Eventually my parents got divorced and Dad ended up marrying Suzanne. My mom eventually remarried, too—a Greek Orthodox doctor. I was able to forgive Suzanne in the end because she loved my father, although the divorce brought me far closer to my mother. She was the one, during those years, who really kept our dreams alive— she'd keep saying things like "You're going to go to college, honey." In many ways, she was the better parent.

And here's the way I ultimately feel: my father made an irretrievably bad decision in terms of what he did with our family. I've always loved him and have always felt like one day he'd come to regret what he'd done—he's just too sensitive a man not to one day look back and feel that way.

Back in Detroit, I fell in again with my old friends. There was this one guy in particular, Joe Klug, and he and I became the de facto leaders of our little group; we were always up to something.

We also always needed money. Joe knew this older guy—he was around twenty-one—who ran this sort of party house a mile or so from our neighborhood; everyone called it "the foosball house" because he had a foosball table in the living room.

The guy was a real thug; he could have had us killed. And he was the kind of a loser who always had younger kids around because he was hoping he could sleep with the girls. So one day when we were all over there, he showed me that he had a ton of mescaline, hundreds of hits, which he was selling. He showed it to me because girls liked me, and he hoped I could facilitate things for him—like if he said he liked a girl, I could go get her and say, "Hey, come with me" and bring her back to his bedroom.

I told Joe about the mescaline, and we decided we were going to steal it. I was sort of a street kid and had a reputation for being very smart and daring and tough. I knew that the act of stealing it would be simple—you just put the shit in a bag and throw it out the window—but that doing it right and not getting caught would be the hard part. I knew we needed a plan.

The deal at this guy's house was that no one could use his bathroom, because it connected to the bedroom where he kept the mescaline. So if you had to use the bathroom, you had to go to a nearby gas station. So one day I told him, "You're not going to get laid if people can't use your bathroom. No girl would think much of a guy who makes you do that." He said, "Really?" He wasn't all that bright.

The brilliance of this plan was that everyone in the neighborhood knew that my friend Joe had to be home at five thirty every night for dinner with his parents. Joe could basically do whatever the hell else he wanted, but dinner at five thirty was written in stone at the Klug house. So one day Joe and I were hanging around the foosball house, playing foosball, listening to music. At a quarter after five, Joe made sure everyone saw him leave. But instead of going home, he just went and waited below the guy's bedroom window, as I'd instructed. A little while later, I acted like I was going to the bathroom but actually slipped down the hall into the bedroom, where I grabbed the mescaline and dropped it out the window to where Joe was waiting. I'd told him, "Don't try to catch it, just let it hit the ground, then pick it up and run like hell back home."

After that, I went to the bathroom and then went back and started playing foosball again. Eventually the guy who lived there went back to his bedroom and realized that his mescaline was gone. I acted like I was just as stunned as he was and actually helped him search everyone who was there. Of course, he couldn't find drugs on anyone. Later I went over to Joe's, where we split the haul. I was pretty proud of myself: I remember telling Joe, "I can out-hood the hoods."

The craziest part of it all is that when that guy needed to buy more mescaline because he had all these people wanting it, I told him, "I know someone who might be able to sell you some." But I wanted to get him desperate so that I could jack up the price, so I made him wait awhile. Then I had a friend sell the mescaline right back to him. I never got caught, and the guy was killed in a car accident twenty years later, so it's safe to say I'm off the hook on that one.

But at the same time all that was going on, I secretly wanted to be an actor, and a plan started taking shape in my mind. I had seen movies like *Taxi Driver, Close Encounters of the Third Kind,* and *The Deer Hunter.* I had read a book about James Dean and a biography of Montgomery Clift that made me even more fascinated by the prospect of pursuing an acting career. It was really *Taxi Driver* that did it, though: my dad and Uncle Barry took me to see it when I was thirteen, and halfway through, my dad whispered to my uncle, "We shouldn't have brought Tommy to this." But I didn't agree. The movie blew me away. I've now seen it more than thirty times. And there was something about the alienation and beauty of actors like Montgomery Clift, Marlon Brando, and James Dean that captivated me. Still, it was more than reverence that I had for them: I somehow already identified with them and saw myself as being at their level. It's hard to explain how this was true, but basically, my life had always felt heightened to a degree—even as a kid my life felt very dramatic, and because I was sort of simultaneously wild but very together, I knew people gossiped about me. And I had a sort of anger that I didn't know what to do with, and acting felt like it could be a way I could creatively channel it.

My high school girlfriend actually coerced me into trying out for a play, and I thought I'd be teased to death for it. But I wasn't, and from there I started singing tenor in musicals staged by local the-ater groups: *Joseph and the Amazing Technicolor Dreamcoat, HMS Pinafore,* and *The Music Man.* I didn't get the lead in *The Music Man* and was just in the chorus—I played a salesman in the opening train scene and also a townsperson—but the director, halfway through the rehearsal process, said, "I should have given you the lead." I said, "Yeah, you should have; the lead isn't any good." I know it sounds like a cliché, but it's like a light had gone on in me by that point: I'd found my calling. The summer after that, I played Conrad Birdie in a Grosse Pointe Players production of *Bye Bye Birdie,* which was a big deal in Detroit and gave me a great deal of confidence. Of course, my deci-sion to be an actor was not a popular one with my parents. But at the same time, I was still kind of wild, and they were happy I'd found something I wanted to do. Also, eventually my dad appreciated the amount of reading that a serious theater student had to do, and he always maintained that if I didn't succeed as an actor, I would none-theless receive a great education.

I didn't exactly spread it around that I had acting ambitions, though. This was Detroit, and acting wasn't a "man's job." Besides, I had connections at General Motors, so to speak, not at Paramount, so I knew that it wouldn't, on a certain level, sound remotely realistic to anyone else. And back then I was interested in being the wonder boy—the straight-A student and athlete—and I really was for a long time. I made everybody feel better. I came from a background where I had a lot of environmental and societal pressures, but I handled it all well. Until, of course, I didn't.

But that was much, much later.

CHAPTER 2

JUST TRY AND STOP ME

WHEN I LEFT home for college at seventeen, I thought I'd never come back. But I ended up leaving Michigan State after less than a year. It just wasn't my cup of tea. I like cities, and East Lansing, Michigan, isn't much of one. I think Woody Allen once said that he feels comfortable in a place where there's a hospital around if you get in a car accident, and I feel the same way. But I also think, in retrospect, that it was when I was at Michigan State that I had my first protracted depression. I remember sitting in room 2A of Armstrong Hall and thinking that my boyhood was over and that even though the last five years of it had been mostly terrible, I still didn't feel ready to be a man. When I decided to leave school, I took the money my dad had given me to pay tuition and hitchhiked to Florida with my friend Doug.

I was doing some crazy things back then; I wasn't serious yet. One night shortly after I'd dropped out, I went to a Led Zeppelin concert with my friend Clyde, and he had hash oil with him. I'd never tried

anything like that before, but we smoked it and drank a fifth of Southern Comfort. And let me tell you, we lost our minds. We were walking
into Detroit's Cobo Hall and I said to Clyde, "Do you think people can
tell that I can't walk?" He said, "You're doing fine—just keep walking."

When we got to our seats, we realized they sucked. We were
kids—we couldn't get good tickets—but we wanted to be able to see
the band. We saw that there was a railing with about a fifty-foot drop
on the other side and figured out that if we could make it over and
down, we'd be in the area where you could actually see the band. So
that's what we decided to do.

I shimmied under the railing and thought I would fall on my feet,
but instead I landed on my back. Clyde was right behind me, and
within seconds of him making it over the police were there. They arrested Clyde. I somehow managed to get away, but as I ran to the
bathroom, I felt a throbbing in my wrist. I'd broken it badly. I ended up
having to go to the hospital later that night, and I was quite dramatic
when I got there. I asked the doctor, "I just want to see my mom—am
I going to die?" The doctor said, "No, you've hurt your arm; you're not
going to die." My mom came to get me, and she was very serious. I
think she saw this accident as symbolic of the direction my life was
taking. She said to me, "Tommy, you've got to do something about
your life; you have so much going for you." I swear to God, that's the
night I mentally became an actor. I knew she was right; something
snapped inside me and I started right then to focus.

My dad was practicing law by then, but he'd gotten an apartment
on the Wayne State University campus back when he'd taught there
and had kept the place. One day I was over there and we had a big
fight that ended with him throwing me out. But as I stormed down
the street, he ran after me, and when he caught up we just happened
to be standing in front of the Wayne State Theater Department. He

told me that the theater department there was good—better than it was at Michigan State, anyway—and I decided to enroll. From that moment on, I was a machine. I took twenty-five credits a semester and started getting straight A's again. I was Phi Beta Kappa, and I starred in most of the plays.

It was around the time that other people started to talk to me about my acting—to notice that I had promise. There was an acting coach there named Tony Schmidt who took me aside one day and said, "You need to understand something: you are very good at this, and I think you should take it seriously." He told me he never said that kind of thing to students, since taking acting seriously as a career isn't usually practical, but he felt compelled to tell me I should pursue it. He said, "Over time, you'll discover that if you go to the right place where the right fight is being fought, which is New York City, the cream rises to the top." He also told me that I needed to always remember that there was a time when all the great actors wanted to be in movies and weren't. He said, "You're one of the rare people—the only kid here—that I could see being in movies like Robert De Niro is in movies. I could see you doing that level of work because of your abilities already." That was an amazing thing to hear.

Some of what I was doing at Wayne State was beginning to get noticed by the local press. I remember that the *Philadelphia Inquirer* called this wild turn I did in the Tennessee Williams play *The Glass Menagerie* "enthusiastically ludicrous." I also starred in *Waiting for Godot* and *A Christmas Carol.* I honestly really was the star of Wayne, and it was a wonderful time in my life. I had my first real girlfriend, Anne Pringle, who was essentially the female star of the school, and we had an apartment a few blocks off campus.

But I also knew that I still wanted to hone my craft. At the time, Temple University in Philadelphia had, apart from Yale, probably the strongest graduate theater department in the country. It was part of something called the League of Professional Theatre Training Programs, which was started by Robert Brustein, who founded Yale Repertory Theatre. As far as I was concerned, the best actors of our time had come out of the program—people like William Hurt, Kevin Kline, Meryl Streep, and Robin Williams.

The concept was to train an American actor to be able to do everything from Shakespeare to what's called kitchen-sink drama—Sam Shepard's plays are an example—to film. The program was established in twelve schools—including Yale, Juilliard, Temple, Brandeis, the University of California, San Diego, the University of Washington at Seattle, and Southern Methodist University—and they would hold auditions in New York, Chicago, Los Angeles, and New Orleans over the course of five months for some fourteen thousand applicants. Things are different now; Temple University's theater program is largely overshadowed by others. But back then, Walt Cherry—a famous Australian theater director—had come to Temple and built an incredible theater program by bringing under one roof five of the best collegiate or graduate school teachers in the world. Eventually the collision of egos caused everything there to fall apart, but that was long after I left.

I'll never forget my audition. I showed up at the Palmer House, a big hotel in Chicago, and was completely overwhelmed: they had three floors reserved for the auditions, and it seemed like there were about a thousand actors there, all vying for these same few spots. I had a private audition with Cherry, after which, I assumed, the teachers would talk to me. So I walked up to their desk and stood there waiting. One of the teachers looked at me coldly and asked, "What is it you want?" I was twenty years old and intimidated as hell. I tried to talk, but nothing came out of my mouth, so he just said, "Well then, go back to your tribe." That was my introduction to high-end acting: "Go back to your tribe."

I wasn't entirely sure what he meant by that, but I got the sense that he considered me among the mediocre, the common—something I had always been terrified of being. I ended up becoming friends with that teacher, and I never asked him about the day of my audition, but I did discover that he was an alcoholic and had a lot of issues. In the end, like so many things, it probably said more about him than it did about me.

Just about the only other thing I ever thought about when I was at Temple was a girl named Michelle Stern. I met her the first day of school and thought I'd never seen a more beautiful girl in my life. I guess we'd all been sent pictures of our future classmates before the semester started, but I had never opened the packet. She obviously did, though, because she walked up to me and said, "I'm Michelle. You're Tom, right?" I was transfixed.

That day, we each had to perform monologues. Although she wasn't very good—she hadn't acted much at all—she had the most amazing body I'd ever seen. Later, a bunch of us had dinner, and when she and I were talking, I asked her, "Can I tell you something?" She said something kind of obnoxious, like "Oh, are you going to tell me I'm pretty?" And I said, "Well, you are really beautiful, but also, you were sort of disastrous in your monologue." She laughed. She knew she was pretty raw. She'd never really acted before and hadn't done a play until her junior year in college.

I was thrilled when I wound up at her apartment later that night. I think some guys are afraid of girls who are really beautiful, but I wasn't. I just desired her in a really profound way. My whole body got hard—not just my dick. But I didn't want to appear too eager because I was trying to play it kind of cool. But then she whispered something in my ear, and I just flew off the couch and tore off my clothes, and she thought that was funny. We both started laughing and then fell in a sort of joyful embrace on her couch. It really was an outrageously erotic night for both of us, and we didn't actually get out of bed for about a day and a half. It was only at that point that she told me that she had a boyfriend in Cincinnati, and she was in love. But I stayed in her life, and by the following summer she confessed that she was in love with me. The eighteen months that followed that summer were probably the happiest of my life; it was the first time that I really, truly fell in love, and I don't know if there's any better feeling in the world.

As a student at Temple I became completely immersed in becoming an actor. Thinking back on it now, I don't know how I managed to become obsessed with something that, let's face it, is so outrageously unrealistic to do with your life. But it was all I thought about. And I got a lot of encouragement. Faculty members would tell me that I was the best actor who'd been through the school in years.

Graduate school taught me a great deal. I studied primarily with Dugald MacArthur, who was one of the better teachers there and thoroughly groomed me. I still remember all of my teachers—people like Joe Leonardo, who worked with actors on vocal production, and Kathy Garinella, who was a movement teacher. I also learned how to build sets and took a theater history class with Walt Cherry, the head of the program, and another one with a brilliant theater historian named Michael Burton.

I was the only first-year student to perform on the main stage there, when I played a rabbi in *The Portage to San Cristóbal of A.H.*—a play adapted from a novel by George Steiner. I had to learn Hebrew for the role, and I ended up studying it with a rabbi named Cohen at a synagogue in Philadelphia. I liked Rabbi Cohen so much that I actually enrolled in Hebrew school at his temple, Society Hill Synagogue; I went to that Hebrew school for six months, when I was done with my acting classes for the day. The kids in that school, who were all thirteen-year-olds studying for their bar mitzvahs, thought it was weird that there was this twenty-two-year-old non-Jew there, but I befriended one named Isaac. And I actually seriously toyed with the idea of converting to Judaism and going and living on a kibbutz in Israel. Michelle was Jewish, and even though she wasn't all that religious, her parents were, and we knew that if we were going to get married we'd have to talk about something like that anyway.

When I wasn't studying Hebrew or in my classes, I was learning about movies. I focused on actors who had a presence that made you say, "I'm willing to continue to watch this even though they're talking about banal shit." I remember seeing the Robert De Niro–Meryl Streep movie *Falling in Love* and not liking the movie but knowing that I was watching two actors who were as good as they get and at the height of their powers. It barely mattered to me that I didn't like the movie: watching them do anything was magnetic.

Another movie that came out when I was in graduate school was *The Big Chill*. I was blown away. I thought William Hurt was auspiciously great, and so to see him act alongside Tom Berenger, JoBeth Williams, Glenn Close, Jeff Goldblum, Meg Tilly, and Kevin Kline—who I've always thought is easily one of the ten best living actors—was exhilarating. I was amazed by the talent but also by the movie in general. It was about such a specific type of feeling—that sense that you're no longer young but you're not old, either, and that everything you know about life is being called into question. I felt like I was right there with them—at a point where dying seemed very far away, but, in a way, youth did, too.

The whole time I was in Philadelphia I knew that it was only a matter of time before I'd go to New York. I understood that that's where I was going to have to be to actually launch an acting career and I was smart enough to understand that I didn't have the where-withal to go there until I'd gotten my MFA. Michelle felt the same way, and we decided to make the move together. And even though I was still deeply in love with her, I also had a feeling of dread about our future because I knew that in order to make it as an actor I probably wasn't going to be able to make all the compromises that would be necessary to maintain our relationship. And becoming successful as an actor meant everything in the world to me. Still, we found a place in Cobble Hill in Brooklyn and got ready for our lives to start.

WE MOVED TO New York on July 1, 1986, just a few weeks before the so-called Preppy Murder, when Robert Chambers strangled Jennifer Levin in Central Park after leaving a bar on the Upper East Side. I don't know why that event sticks out in my head so much but I think it probably has to do with the fact that this violent murder seemed to be in such stark contrast to the cushion of hopefulness that I felt like I was living in. New York was big and full of possibilities. I don't think I realized just how big it was until I looked at the phone book one day, saw that there were something like 12 million names in there, and realized I didn't know one of them. At Temple, I'd been a big star, and on top of that, Michelle and I both had all the exuberance of youth. But we had no connections at all in the real-life acting world and we didn't know how to get them.

It was tough in the beginning. I had read in *Backstage* magazine about how the Ensemble Studio Theatre was where David Mamet and Lanford Wilson launched their new works, so I started taking acting classes there. I felt like I was a freshman in college again. I would do menial chores just to get the chance to dress the stage. And it was worth it. This was a place that had been started by Curt Dempster, who was both a playwright and an actor. He was friends with some of the world's best playwrights, both those who were already established and those who were coming up—from David Mamet and Horton Foote to John Patrick Shanley. Curt would decide to, say, put on *Cyrano de Bergerac;* he would play Cyrano and then hire out other New York actors to play the smaller parts. A lot of talented actors came up through Ensemble—people like John Turturro, Ellen Barkin, William H. Macy, and Richard Dreyfuss—and plays would often launch there before moving to Broadway.

I could tell that Ensemble was the place to be, but at the same time, I was a realist. I'd look around my acting classes, just like every actor does, and think, "Not all of us are going to be in movies—in fact, the odds are that none of us are going to be in movies—so I'd better be the best actor in this fucking class if I'm to continue to do this with any possibility of it being real." I was determined.

It was an exciting time to be in New York. I remember I'd walk out of the four-story brownstone apartment building Michelle and I lived in and think that it didn't matter which way I turned, because a walk in either direction was going to be interesting. But New York's a tough place. Mike Wallace really embodied the city for me. I'd watch *60 Minutes* and think, "This motherfucker *is* New York City—his whole comportment, how bright and thorough he is, the way he takes everyone to task about everything, and his generosity and his coldness." New York is a mess of contradictions.

I was doing everything I knew I had to do to succeed—whether that was hundreds of push-ups every day to stay in shape or obsessively reading Shakespeare plays. Sometimes it felt like I was trapped in a cycle I'd never escape: I wanted to be in movies so it was like, okay, how do you get in a movie? Well, you get a tape of you being in a movie. Well, how do you get the first tape then? The logic would spin round and round like a washing machine.

In New York City back then, if you didn't have an agent, you'd go to the Actors' Equity Association, located at Forty-Fourth Street and Broadway, which was the union for actors and stage managers, because they listed the open calls for theater auditions. If you saw, say, an open call for *The Tooth of Crime* by Sam Shepard, you'd sign up and sit there for two and a half days to get an audition. I'd go there about once a week, on Tuesdays.

Because I had to manage my time carefully in New York, between leaving my apartment in the morning and not coming back until nighttime, I started playing chess with the newspaper when I was waiting around at Actor's Equity. One day, some big Italian guy walked up to me and said, "Tired of playing with yourself? Because I am." It was James Gandolfini, who later, of course, gained fame starring in HBO's *The Sopranos*. Actors who are that good are usually very bright and funny, and Jimmy is no exception.

I was also seeing a lot of theater and getting a strong sense of which actors who were already making it were legitimately great. I saw John Malkovich do *True West* with Gary Sinise on Broadway, and he was magnificent. When I saw him play Biff opposite Dustin Hoffman in *Death of a Salesman,* I saw how *really* good he was. But at the same time—and I realize how conceited this sounds—I thought I was just as good, if not better, than the biggest actors out there. I don't think I would have continued to pursue acting in the dogged way that I was if I didn't believe that. I understood that if I made it, it wasn't going to be because I was pretty; I just believed in my raw talent. Of course, you can't be objective about yourself, but something in me still believed that I was as good as the actors I was watching, and that made me continue to pursue it even though I wasn't getting anywhere.

At the time I was doing odd jobs like loading trucks for UPS and Coca-Cola and working at nightclubs. It was when I was working at the clubs that I started to see people doing a lot of drugs. I was curious about them, but I wasn't doing any of that myself really. Jack Kerouac, Bob Dylan, John Lennon, Chet Baker—all my cultural heroes had been somehow connected to drugs, so I believe I had a constant back-of-my-mind fixation with the dark side. I was highly aware of the fact that in the sixties, all the guys who were considered cool were drugging and they always had all the girls. But I also wanted to be the best actor in my class, and that kept me from living anything but a fairly clean life. I wanted my acting teachers to keep telling me that they thought I was going to be a star, so I wasn't going to get all fucked-up at night and then go to acting class hungover in the morning.

For three years, I worked at a catering company called Great Performances, which would handle functions like home dinner parties hosted by wealthy New Yorkers. The food would be pre-prepared by a great cook who would show up with a staff of waiters in tuxedos, and we would serve the dinner. Every actor in town wanted to work there. Your day was over by one o'clock, which meant that you had the rest of your day free for possible auditions. You had to get to work at four in the morning so everything would be ready to roll two hours later, but that was a small price to pay.

I worked there for three years. At the time, they had a contract for the executive dining rooms of the Port Authority at the World Trade Center and at Kennedy Airport. I spent most of my time at the World

Trade Center. I didn't like working at the parties. I felt jealous of the rich people, and some of them treated us horribly. Nasty nouveau riche women would tell me that my pants weren't long enough and that I had to go home to change; I'd go sit down somewhere, then come back in the same fucking pants and they'd say, "Oh, those are perfect." It was bullshit.

Even in that job I was ambitious, and decided I had to be the featured waiter in the executive dining room. My boss there—a lovely African-American gentleman named Ken Stiles—ran the executive dining room and had been doing it for fifteen years at that point. If I had an audition at 12:30 P.M., he'd let me go early and then pretend he had to send me out to do an errand; that way no one from Port Authority could get on my case for not being there.

Eventually, I did become the featured waiter. By then Michelle was working as a hostess at Fafi, a restaurant in Brooklyn Heights. But a year and a half into our life in New York, we were still working these server jobs. Moreover, I was starting to feel less passionate about our relationship.

In the spring of 1987, at an audition for a Sam Shepard play, *Cowboy Mouth,* I met a pretty, red-haired, very talented girl named Tisha Roth. There were just two people in this play—Sam and Patti Smith played the parts initially—and Tisha got the female part. I didn't get the male one, but I was so mesmerized by her, I almost didn't care. I was also doing another play at the time—*The Indian Wants the Bronx* at the Manhattan Theatre Club. Tisha had been working at the Williamstown Theatre Festival, at Williams College—it was where all of the seriously talented people went; Christopher Walken was also there that summer. Tisha was considered one of the best actresses there.

After Tisha and I met, we started spending a lot of time together.

I hadn't been with anybody but Michelle for nearly five years—hadn't even kissed anybody else—but when I met Tisha, my attraction to Michelle began to cool. I was confused because up until that point I'd pretty much assumed I'd stay with Michelle forever.

One night at Tisha's apartment, we began fooling around. I broke down, though, because I felt so guilty about Michelle—I literally started crying. Tisha was very concerned and asked me what was wrong. I didn't know how to explain it.

I didn't know—and I still don't—how people fall out of love with each other. It really is one of the great mysteries of adulthood. And after that night with Tisha, I was trying to make sense of my feelings around all of this. I was writing a lot in my journal, and then Tisha and I started exchanging letters. And here's what an idiot I am: I liked the letters I was writing her so much that I photocopied them. They weren't love letters—they were mostly about why I felt like I couldn't just jump into a relationship with her because I didn't know when I'd be emotionally ready to do that again. This letter writing went on for several months.

In late May of that year, Michelle found all the letters. And she read every fucking word of them. When I came home that day, she said, "You have to move the fuck out." She didn't know who Tisha was, and she didn't care. She just said it was clear that I was in love with somebody else, and I had to go.

I was in deep shock. I'd kept the letters behind my dresser in our bedroom, in an envelope taped to the back. They were very well hidden. But she was cleaning some area where she never cleaned and found them. And when Michelle was done, she was done. She didn't care that kicking me out was going to make her life harder. I honestly hadn't known she had that kind of strength until she did that.

It was terrible. I had loved our life and our little apartment on

Clinton and Degraw, two blocks from Atlantic Avenue, in Brooklyn. Michelle understood that I wasn't great with directions and that this was the only part of New York I knew, so she called the landlord of our building and asked if he had any other apartments in the area; he did, and she found me a new place the very next day. I was inconsolable, but she was very matter-of-fact about everything, and in fact packed up all my stuff. She didn't let the kind of shape I was in prevent what had to happen. I begged her to let me stay, but she just wasn't hearing it. Within four days she had me packed up and moved. Not only that, but she'd also found me furniture, bought me toiletries and cleaning supplies, and hired the movers.

I moved two and a half blocks from Michelle but she wouldn't see me at all. Still, she was such a good person that she wanted to keep track of me until she knew I was going to be okay. Of course, I wasn't okay for a while—I cried for a year and could barely get through my life at all in the first six months.

I realized I had to go home, to Michigan—to my mom. I took a leave of absence from the catering job and stayed with my mom for two months. And once I was there, I was so disconsolate that I didn't get out of bed for twelve days. Finally my mother said, "You have to get over the sadness. You have an apartment back in New York—you signed a lease there." My dad came over and told me, "I know you're afraid you'll never fall in love again, but you will." And then my mom said something I'd never heard from her: "I know that I didn't support this idea of you being an actor six years ago, but I do now. Because you're good at it and you're only going to improve."

At a certain point, I started to feel a little better. My interest in Tisha had been completely obliterated by my desire to get back with Michelle, but while I was home, I reconnected with a girl that I'd had a dalliance with in high school, and being with her—being with someone besides Michelle—wasn't as jarring as I'd thought it was going to be. That helped me. Looking back, it's hard to believe that I was so concerned with being with someone new. If only I knew then that there would come a time when I'd want to be with somebody new *every hour*.

One day my mom walked in and said, "Pack, because you're going back to New York tomorrow." And I did it. I went back to Cobble Hill. Of course, I was still trying desperately to get Michelle back, but she wouldn't hear of it.

And yet out of this horrible depression came renewed vigor and ambition. At this point I was twenty-four, and I knew my odds of making it as an actor were still slim. But I was also getting a sense of my own abilities, and I felt in a lot of ways that I'd just tapped into those abilities. I was cast in a one-act Arthur Miller play alongside people who a year before I'd thought were very good. Now I was working with them and thinking, "I need to be working with better people." The director was a Broadway big shot who told me, "You're working at a higher level than your co-actors, and you need to know that. You need to carry this play. That's the only way it will work." When that play was over, I was moved up to the master acting class at Ensemble.

Not long after that, I was sitting in the waiting room of Phoenix Artists, waiting for a meeting with an agent, and I started talking to a charming, sweet aspiring actress who was also there. She got called in before me, and when I came out of my own meeting an hour later, she was there waiting for me. Her name was Edie Falco.

Edie and I decided to go to a Mexican restaurant on Sixteenth Street and Eighth Avenue called Mary Ann's. I liked her right away; she also seemed so worldly. I was still hurting from my breakup with

Michelle, but Edie gave me the hope that it was still possible to fall for someone else. We started dating and I took an enormous amount of solace with her; she was very kind to me.

Our sensibilities were fairly similar. I'd say we were both openly miserable but in a sort of bemused way. We liked each other but not enough to take care of the other person's misery—we both knew we had enough misery of our own to worry about.

By then I was living with a friend, Tom Benson, whom I'd met working for Great Performances. I hadn't been able to make the rent on the apartment Michelle had found for me in Brooklyn—it cost seven hundred dollars a month—and I'd started to become almost irrationally worried that I was going to be evicted. Someone at work had put the fear of God into me by telling me that if you get evicted from an apartment in New York, you can never get another apartment for the rest of your life. So I'd started asking around at work, trying to see if anyone was looking for a roommate. Tom told me he had a rent-controlled two-bedroom, third-floor walk-up in the West Village for $219 that he'd inherited from an ex who had left New York. It was on Thirteenth Street and Seventh Avenue, and the minute I saw it I knew I wouldn't leave that place until I could afford to live wherever I wanted. It was a brownstone with high ceilings, in a great part of town, and cost almost nothing.

Edie was living in Brooklyn's Park Slope section with some room-mates, but she started staying with me in my room at Tom's place, and we basically began plotting to try to get him to move out so the two of us could have it for ourselves. She irritated him already and we knew it, so we'd attempt to come up with other ways to bother him. He was a writer, and he liked peace and quiet, so at one point I left the TV on in my room for nine days straight, thinking it would slowly drive him crazy. It did, but when he eventually exploded, instead of leaving he said, "I strongly suggest that you two move into Edie's old place in Park Slope." We didn't, though; we all just stayed where we were.

Edie and I were a funny couple; we both basically believed that we deserved to be big stars and were getting a raw deal because we weren't yet. I have no idea where that sense of entitlement came from, but we assumed we were talented and thought it was a damn shame that the world was slow to catch on to this. She was hilariously focused on us succeeding as actors. We'd be at dinner with people, talking about something or other, and then she'd suddenly interrupt and say, "Hey, Tom, have you come up with any ideas for how we can get jobs as actors where we're actually getting paid? I'm tired of us having to pay to act; I think it should be the other way around." At that point, we were doing these showcases where we'd rent out a space for nine hundred dollars, say, and put on plays and try to get agents to come see them and sign us. We'd make up a bunch of invites and drop them off with at least fifty different agencies in town; then maybe eight of them would show up, and they wouldn't even be the agent but the assistant's assistant's assistant. Then we'd put on our showcase and have everyone in the audience fill out cards—one for each of the actors in it—that showed what they thought of us. The cards were supposed to have two options for them to check: either "call the agency" or "send a picture." But I made the cards so I added a third option—"drop dead." That actually got me more attention than anything else at the showcase: some of the agents who were there laughed when they saw the cards and said, "Who thought of adding 'drop dead'?" Someone would tell them, "Tom Sizemore did," and the agent would turn to me and say, "Hey, that's pretty funny." Whatever it took to get noticed.

When Edie and I went out, I think everyone thought we were crazy. We'd get all dressed up—she'd put on a dress and a hat and we'd talk about how that was probably how Rosanna Arquette would dress;

so it was good to dress like that because Rosanna Arquette was a big star at the time. Then we'd go into restaurants and Edie would say to the waiter, "Do you have any idea who you're waiting on?" The waiter would look at me, look at her, then shrug and say no. Edie would pretend to be aghast. She'd go, "Are you insane? Did you just get out of a monastery?" It was a joke but at the same time we were kind of serious. And I did think she was incredibly talented—the most talented actress I'd ever seen. I saw her in a play that she did with some students from the State University of New York at Purchase, and she was magnificent. Essentially, what Edie and I had in common more than anything was a sort of gallows humor. Some mornings, we'd have to Ro Sham Bo to decide who was going to get out of bed and get the coffee, because we both felt too discouraged.

Edie and I were together for a few years and she introduced me to a lot in that time. She grew up in Northport, Long Island, but had been coming into the city since she was a kid, so she knew Manhattan up and down and showed it to me. She took me to the theater a lot—I remember we saw Will Smith in *Six Degrees of Separation* together. We also drank quite a lot together. But Edie was smart and started hauling herself over to an AA meeting in Greenwich Village. She saw the writing on the wall. Her problem was never drugs—it was alcohol. But the truth is, she fucked a lot better when she drank. She was such a lady, but when she drank, she was like, "Come here and fuck me."

I did all sorts of odd jobs besides waiting tables. I tried telemarketing. I even worked as a bouncer at a strip club. But things started to happen for me, careerwise, faster than they did for Edie. I'd met a casting director named Risa Bramon through the Ensemble Studio Theatre, and she really liked me. Risa had been one of Curt Dempster's first students at Ensemble and eventually she became the casting director for the theater. She did a wonderful job—that woman had an eye for talent—and because of that, she got hired as the casting director on the Madonna film *Desperately Seeking Susan*. That was her big break, and she didn't look back; as a result, she ended up essentially being responsible for bringing all of the great New York actors to Hollywood— Alec Baldwin, John Turturro, Ethan Hawke, Anthony LaPaglia, and Edie among them. Before *Desperately Seeking Susan*, a lot of movies weren't reading actors out of New York, and Risa helped to change that.

Risa brought me in to read for the role of a thief in *Blue Steel*, and not only did I get the part but my scene was with the star of the movie, Jamie Lee Curtis. The project also introduced me to the director Kathryn Bigelow, whom I would work with again in *Point Break* and *Strange Days;* she later won an Oscar for *The Hurt Locker*. Kathryn liked me from the get-go and called up Oliver Stone, who was producing *Blue Steel*, to tell him he should cast me in *Born on the Fourth of July*. I had already read for that film because Risa had brought me in, but Oliver hadn't made a decision yet. But Kathryn's call was all it took: "Tell Sizemore he's cast," he told her.

At the time, Oliver Stone was the biggest, most powerful director in the world. He'd won Oscars for *Platoon* and *Wall Street*. And I was being paid $150,000 and getting to fly to the Philippines to work with him. At that point, I had never been out of the country. When I found out I could go out there early to adjust to the time, the climate, and the set, I got on that plane as quickly as I could.

I flew to the Philippines on January 12, 1989, and had twelve days before I had to shoot anything. I think I was the first one there besides Tom Cruise. Billy Baldwin arrived later; Daniel and Stephen Baldwin were in the movie, too. I knew the Baldwins from New York; Alec and I had the same agent starting out, and I'd even been out to their family's place in Massapequa. I remember being blown away by how damn attractive they all were.

I had some time before I had to work, but I wasn't really interested in hanging out; I was focused on preparing for the movie. We were all in this huge hotel that Ferdinand Marcos had built for his daughter's wedding, in this incredibly poor province. It was beyond third world, aside from that hotel, the kind of place where people used feces— both their own and from animals—as material to build their houses. I took all this in, but again, I was just focused on how this was my shot and I had to do a good job there. While for me movie sets later became places to go on location and party, at this point I was still very much a straight arrow. While I'd smoked pot and drank a little bit, I hadn't done any narcotics yet and what's more, this was a very serious set. I never saw any members of the cast or crew party; I don't think I ever even saw anyone hungover.

I liked to run every morning along the South China Sea. After one such run, very early in the day, I was sitting in the cafeteria writing in my journal. A guy walked up to me and said, "Hey, man, mind if I join you?" I looked up, but I was so exhausted and out of it that I could only really see that there was some guy standing there. I said, "Actually, I would prefer it if you didn't. I'm just sort of focused on what I'm writing." And he went, "Okay, man. I get that. I like that. You're just being yourself, doing your own thing." His voice was funny and distinctive, and I suddenly realized it was Willem Dafoe, who was coming off big roles in *Platoon, The Last Temptation of Christ,* and *Mississippi Burning.* He was huge. I went, "Oh, man—I'm so sorry. Sit down, please." And he just sort of stood there smiling and said, "No, I get it, you're rude. That's your thing. I can respect someone doing their thing. You want me to go back to my room?" I kept apologizing, and he said something along the lines of "What if I wasn't Willem Dafoe but just another schmo?" He was being facetious and giving me shit but in a funny, unique way. I said, "If you make fun of me anymore, I'm going to throw this bowl of rice at you." I guess Kathryn Bigelow, who had directed him in *The Loveless,* had told him to look out for me on the set and showed him my picture, so that's why he'd come up to me. Finally he sat down and said, "No wonder Kathryn likes you; she loves rude people." We became fast friends.

Still, I spent most of the time before I had to shoot anything working on a scene where I would be sitting on the top of a hill in a wheelchair—my character was quadriplegic—yell, "Banzai, motherfucker!" and then go flying down and smash into a bunch of wheelchairs at the bottom. I knew that Oliver wouldn't want to have to use a stuntman and then cut away, so I wanted to figure out a few things—like how I was going to go flying out of a wheelchair while defying my natural human instinct to protect myself by trying to break my fall with my hands. What I came up with was that I'd have to make my hands inaccessible. So I asked this other actor to tie my hands together and then to tie them to my waist with rope. The guy thought I was completely nuts, but I knew I had to get my hands in a place where I simply wouldn't be able to move them. The other part I had to figure out was how I was going to turn my body around in midair so I'd take the blow on my shoulder while having my body remain flaccid. I knew that, as a quadriplegic, all I could move was my nose, so it was complicated as hell figuring all of this out.

The only way I could get it right, I knew, was to practice. But it was so hot there that I couldn't do it until the sun went down. So on ten of those twelve days before shooting, I'd be up there at sunset screaming, "Banzai, motherfucker!" and flying down the hill on my wheelchair and crashing into the others. I got pretty banged up fairly quickly. Apparently Oliver was coming home from the set at one point and saw me doing this on the makeshift hill that had been built. For about ten minutes he watched me come down and smash into chairs and push the wheelchair back up the hill and do it again. I probably did it some six times without having a clue that he was watching. But apparently, after watching for a while, he turned to his first assistant director, Joe Reidy, and asked, "Who is that?" And Joe said, "His name's Tom Sizemore." Oliver asked how long I did this for, and Joe said he didn't know but could find out. So he sent one of his guys over to me to ask. So some guy came running up to me and said, "Sizemore, how long do you do that for? Joe wants to know." I had no idea who Joe was or why he wanted to know; I just shrugged, looked at the sun, which was almost completely gone at that point, and said, "I don't know—till it's completely dark. About an hour and a half, I guess." Apparently that impressed Oliver; he liked that I wasn't afraid. I guess it also impressed Joe—we ended up becoming friends later. Joe's an amazing guy. He's been the first AD not only to Oliver but also to Martin Scorsese and Woody Allen. The first AD really runs the show on a movie set—he's the one who has to say to the director, "We're done, we're moving on," and have the director listen. When the director's someone like Oliver or Marty, that's not always easy, but they always listened to Joe.

Finally it was my first day of working, and I knew I had to hit it out of the park. So I went for it. When I was done, Joe came up to me and told me that Oliver wanted to see me. I went back to see Oliver and he said, "That was good, so we don't even have to do a safety—unless you want to. Oh, hey, you want to watch the playback?" He was very casual—as if we knew each other and hung out all the time. Of course, I didn't have a clue what the hell "playback" or "safety" even meant; I didn't even know what a craft service table was at that point. But I wasn't going to tell him that. "Um, I'll watch playback," I said and he played back my scene on the monitor he had right there.

I had never seen myself on-screen at that point, and I hated it.

My face looked huge on the monitor and really fucked-up. My pores seemed enormous and I had scraggly hair because I'd been told to grow my hair out, but all I could focus on were these huge pores on my nose. I must have had a horrified look on my face—I probably looked like I'd just smelled shit or something—because Oliver asked me what was wrong. I didn't know what to say because I didn't want to tell him I was horrified, so I just mumbled something about how it was just strange because I'd never seen myself act before. And then I sort of shuffled away, saying, "So, great, I'm not going to do a safety. Thanks."

I was still really in my head, and just because Oliver thought I did well didn't mean I believed it. In fact, as I was walking away, I started thinking about how in the scene I actually looked like I knew what was going to happen next. It's a scene where a guy was threatening to kill me, and I didn't really think I sold it; in fact I thought I looked like someone who knew he *wasn't* going to get killed. As I was dwelling on this, I turned to someone on the set and asked, "Hey, what's a safety?" And the crew guy said, "That's when they shoot it again. Run back if you want one, kid." So I ran back to Stone and said, "I've thought about it and I do want a safety." So we did it again, and that's when I really thought I nailed it. Oliver ultimately agreed that the second take was better.

For the next couple of days after that we just shot innocuous stuff. Then, on my fourth day of work, we did the scene where I go careening down the hill on my wheelchair. I had gotten very good at flying through the air and taking the blow on my shoulder but giving the illusion that I was going headfirst into the ground. It went well. Then my character gets into this fight with another vet, who was played by Andrew Lauer. I had decided before we shot that I was going to spit on him even though it wasn't in the script. Andrew ended up spitting back, and we got into this full-on spitting war, which is how Oliver got the idea to have Tom Cruise and Willem Dafoe get into a spitting war later in the movie. Because of that, and I think because he could tell just how passionate I was, Oliver wrote me two more scenes. I ended up staying for twenty-seven days even though I was originally just supposed to be there for two weeks. And while I was there I found out that I was cast in *Lock Up,* a Sylvester Stallone movie I had screen-tested for in Los Angeles on my way to the Philippines. It felt like my whole life was changing overnight.

But first I had to get home, which actually proved difficult because I had to fly to Manila and then stay overnight in Manila before heading back to New York. The revolution had just started there, and I was staying in Manila with Willem, who was flying out to Poland the next day to do a movie called *Triumph of the Will.* Suddenly bombs started going off in the sky, and I became convinced our hotel was going to be overrun. I was terrified and kept running over to Willem's hotel room and waking him up. But nothing happened to us, and I was able to get on a plane back to New York the next day as planned.

Almost as soon as I got back to New York I had to go to Los Angeles. I was willing to go to L.A. as much as I needed to—I didn't care where my acting career happened as long as it happened—but Edie was dead set against leaving New York. And that's when Edie and I began having problems. We were young and I was away a lot. And even though I ultimately fell in love with her, I was never all the way in emotionally. I just don't think I had fully recovered from Michelle.

But suddenly the work was coming, and it was coming fast. I did a movie called *Rude Awakening* and then *Lock Up,* which introduced me to both Stallone and Mickey Rourke. Mickey's talent just blew me away. When I had seen him in *Diner* I realized there was someone in movies who was doing things that had never been done before. And when we met I think we bonded over the fact that neither of us was quite right. There was also something very charismatic about him; he was Marlon Brando and didn't know it. Everything about him was interesting: the way he walked—he had that pigeon-toed walk—and the way he looked and the sweetness he had underneath it all. Mickey and I are both weird. He's had four dogs, all named Loki, and when each one dies, he names the next one that. I think we both want to talk to each other more, but we're both chickens. He likes to talk to whichever Loki is around, and I like to talk to books.

Anyway, I made seventy-five thousand dollars on *Lock Up,* and I took the money I was supposed to use for a hotel stay and instead moved into the Oakwood—a furnished-apartment complex between Burbank and Hollywood, which is usually filled with child actors who are trying to get their big break—because it only cost eight hundred dollars a month. That meant I pocketed another forty thousand in per diem. I was very conscious back then about how much I needed to get by—I think I was still paranoid after hearing that you could never get another apartment once you got evicted in New York. I did not want to go back to waiting tables.

Stallone really liked me. He was the first big star I ever met, and I have to say I've still never met anyone better adjusted to stardom. He's a good father, has been with the same woman, his wife, Jennifer Flavin, for nearly twenty-five years, and is simply the nicest guy you could meet. He basically decided I was a good actor and took me over to Creative Artists Agency (CAA), where he introduced me to Ron Meyer, who was one of the founders. Ron then took me over to meet with Bryan Lourd and Kevin Huvane. At the time, they were just kids my age but they ended up becoming the "Young Turks" along with Richard Lovett, who sort of ran that group, and Jay Maloney, who, tragically, ended up killing himself. I could tell that they were brutally ambitious—like me.

I'd always known I was ambitious, but this was around when I realized just how competitive I was. My attitude about auditioning became: If you beat me today, I'm going to come back tomorrow and beat you. The fact of the matter is that if you can imagine yourself being anything else but an actor, then you should be doing that other thing. Acting has to be your calling because regardless of how successful you are or how soon you get that success, you're going to have times when there's something you want that you're not going to get, no matter who you are. And that hurts. Because you're not selling Girl Scout cookies. You're selling you. So if you don't get the job—well, you can obfuscate it with all kinds of bullshit if you want to, but it's a personal rejection. It's the *most* personal kind of rejection. So you have to have a very thick skin and a very deep belief in yourself to get through that. I developed a system around this time, which was to let myself grieve for the twenty-four hours after I didn't get something, then say, "Fuck it" and move on.

One of the starring roles I got early on was in a movie called *A Matter of Degrees,* written by Randy Poster, whose sister, Meryl Poster, was already a bigwig at Miramax and who had gone to Brown University, in Providence, Rhode Island, where we were shooting, with John F. Kennedy Jr. Now, my family was completely obsessed with the Kennedys, so when someone told me that Randy was friends with John, I didn't believe it. I asked Randy and he said it was true, then offered to call him to prove it. So he called up John-John and handed the phone to me. That's when I heard this voice that was unmistakably his say, "I understand you don't actually believe I'm Randy's friend. Well, I'll prove it to you because I'm going to be on the set tomorrow, doing a scene where I play the guitar and have one line."

I guess John-John did a play at Brown, and his mother, Jackie Kennedy Onassis, came to see it, but she told him afterward, "I do not approve of you doing this because it is not a serious pursuit—in the memory of your father and your uncle Bobby, I don't want you to go through your public life as a pretender." But he agreed to take this tiny, one-line role in the movie not only because he was friends with Randy but also because his girlfriend at the time, Christina Haag, was in it.

When John got to the set, I was standing at an elevator by myself wearing my costume, which was a pair of overalls because I played a guy who restores cars. I heard a banging noise getting closer down the hall behind me and as I turned around I said, "Who's the cripple?" And there was John-John, hobbling up on crutches because he'd hurt his leg in a skiing accident and had just had knee surgery. He had a big smile on his face and said, "Are you referring to me? That's not very nice, Tom."

It blew my mind, first, that it was him, and second, that he knew my name. I was sort of speechless but he just added, "You should be careful before you go around shouting things like that; one day you might say it to an actual cripple and that might be uncomfortable." I just stood there, nodding sort of dumbly. I had pressed the button on the elevator, but no light went on so I just assumed it was broken, but then John reached out with his crutch and pressed it and the light suddenly flicked on. I remember thinking, "He's so magnetic that he has the ability to make broken elevators work." He was extremely nice and we became good friends.

When he reached his arm out with his crutch, it was the most built arm I'd ever seen, and I thought to myself, "I want my arm to look like that." He told me that he didn't much go to the gym. "I go to the gym to use the steam room," he said. "New York City's my gym." He explained that he'd Rollerblade or skateboard to Central Park and then play football or Frisbee there and do chin-ups on buildings that he passed where they were doing construction. It sounds silly, but that really inspired me, and I started doing a workout routine where I throw a football against a wall outside; it's a routine I keep up to this day.

Randy came over and said, "What'd I tell you? Now do you believe me?" and the three of us just laughed. John shot the scene where he played guitar and then later he watched me do a scene. And we actually hung out a little after that: I played football with him in Central Park a few times and went out to dinner with him and his friends. One night he invited me out with people who were involved in his magazine, *George*. I felt uncomfortable, because I didn't really fit in or know what they were talking about, and he just suddenly said to everyone, "Hey, let's stop talking about *George* because it's got to be boring for Tom." He was that kind of a guy: he was very compassionate and had the sort of presence that naturally made people want to follow. I have to admit that meeting and befriending him was incredibly exciting. It might sound ridiculous but it was one of the best things that happened to me when I first started out as an actor. I was devastated when he died; he was a remarkable man.

This is around when I signed with a manager named Suzan Bymel. She was friends with a filmmaker named Jill Goldman, who was putting together her first movie, a romantic drama titled *Love Is Like That* (later changed to *Bad Love*). I was basically told, "Hey, Jill Goldman's really rich, and if you go through the rehearsal process for the movie, she'll foot the bill for you to live at the Chateau Marmont while you shoot it." So I went through the rehearsal process, she did end up putting me up at the Chateau, and the movie became one of my favorite roles of all time. I played this passionate loser named Lenny who falls for this girl when she comes into the gas station where he's working.

They have money problems, as well as relationship problems, and they end up scheming to rob a fading movie star the woman works for. It was a small movie, but I loved playing a romantic lead—especially opposite Pamela Gidley, who was a big model at the time. While I was shooting *Love Is Like That* I landed a recurring role in the CBS drama *China Beach*—which starred Dana Delaney and was about a U.S. military hospital during the Vietnam War, and in which Dana Delaney played the head nurse—as Sergeant Vinnie Ventresca, a wounded sergeant from Brooklyn who handles the mine-sniffing dogs.

Around then, Bryan Lourd basically said to me, "I need you to be in L.A. now for work." And my attitude was "Great—I'll be there next week." The way I looked at it was this: I had worked my ass off for ten years to get opportunities, and now that I was going to be getting some, I didn't want to miss a single one. I think Edie was miffed by how easily I made the decision to leave New York, but a real decision is when you weigh one possibility against another and this was no decision: I just said yes, knowing it was the right thing to do. Even though Edie and I had a huge fight about the whole thing, she helped me pack and even agreed to ship the stuff I couldn't take with me. (However, I realized I'd be leaving her with literally nothing if I took the bed and the couch and all the rest of the furniture, so I ended up just taking my books.)

First I went to Chicago to make a movie called *Watch It,* and then, on May 1, 1991, I moved to L.A., into an apartment on Harratt Street in West Hollywood. I really liked my driver on *Watch It,* a guy named Scott Silver, and he was always talking about how he wanted to be a screenwriter. So I told him that if he wanted to move out to L.A., he could live with me. On set, I also became better friends with John McGinley. The two of us would joke about how I lived in a Hollywood mansion. I think Scott really believed that that was what he was going to be moving into when he decided to come out, but it was just a two-bedroom condo. Scott enrolled in the American Film Institute and lived with me the whole time. He ended up making it as a screenwriter, too; in 2011, he was nominated for an Oscar for his script for *The Fighter*.

I didn't like L.A. all that much but L.A. was liking me. I suddenly had a million dollars to burn. But I was pretty careful with it. I wanted to get a Porsche, for example, but instead I got a Mustang—though I did end up later getting a Porsche. I have never cared all that much about things—possessions—although sometimes I get a little superstitious. For instance, I had this certain pair of jeans that I was wearing when I got my first job, and so I started to believe that I had to wear them on every audition or job meeting I went to or else I wouldn't get the part. This pair of jeans got to be disgusting—completely ripped up and tattered—and I seriously looked like some kind of a grunge kid in them. But I kept wearing them.

It was getting to the point that before I'd even finish a job, I had another one, and in a way I never had time to really sit down and think about what was happening. I did a small comedic role in *Point Break* and played a bank president in *Harley Davidson and the Marlboro Man*—my second time working with Mickey Rourke.

The amazing thing is that I wasn't being pigeonholed at all. I was being used for both drama and comedy and I could go from playing a romantic lead in *Love Is Like That* to playing a gay serial killer in *Where Sleeping Dogs Lie,* with Sharon Stone. But it's not like I was getting everything I tried out for. I auditioned some six times for the part of Mr. Pink in *Reservoir Dogs*. It came down to Steve Buscemi or me, and they wanted me to go to Sundance in Colorado and workshop it before they'd even cast me. Obviously they cast Buscemi.

What I remember above all from that period is that on every

movie, the director would pull me aside for dinner or a talk and tell me that I should be aware that I had an incredible ability, and that I should never lose sight of it because I could become one of the greatest actors who ever lived. But I never dwelled on those things; I didn't know how to handle hearing something like that. So I'd just go on to the next project.

CHAPTER 3

MAKING IT

ONE OF MY FIRST leading roles was in a movie called *Passenger 57,* but honestly, what was most memorable about that entire experience was that it introduced me to Elizabeth Hurley. I remember when I first saw her, four days into the movie, at the table read in Orlando, Florida: I'd never seen a girl that beautiful in my life. She had stunningly flawless ivory skin, a beautiful voice, and a charming throaty laugh.

Wesley Snipes, whom I'd known for a long time and was one of the stars of the film, saw her at the same time. He looked at me and said, "You can have the black girl," meaning the actress who was playing the other stewardess. I saw that he might be serious about hitting on Elizabeth so right then I walked across the room to where Elizabeth was at a table getting a brownie or something. I started to introduce myself to her and she said, "I know who you are." I think I stammered out, "What?" And she said, "I'm in room 219 and you're in room 119. It's on the cast list."

I said something like "I have to apologize but I'm kind of a neo-phyte when it comes to talking to women as beautiful as you." And she said, "A neophyte? I love you." I laughed and said, "It's that easy?" and she said, "I'm sorry, I meant that I love the fact that you know the word *neophyte*." I laughed and asked her to dinner, explaining that I was a neophyte at that, too.

Later that night, we went to an Italian restaurant in central Florida, then went back to her room and drank wine and listened to the Beatles; we just kind of cuddled and sang the songs to each other and hung out, and then I went home. I didn't even try to kiss her. I felt like she was just too pretty to kiss. To me, her beauty blocked everything out. It was actually really unhealthy because I let her beauty keep me in a subordinate position. I literally couldn't conceal my awe or worshipful feelings for her.

The next day she came by my room and said, "Come on, we're going to get some magazines and books." We drove to a Borders, and she bought *Madame Bovary* and a bunch of other books; I was impressed. That night we went back to her hotel room, which had a little kitchenette, and she made roasted chicken with green beans and broke out two bottles of wine. I think I was in love by the time I had my second glass. Then she went into the bedroom and came out in lingerie that would make her later outfits in the *Austin Powers* movies seem tame, and she got on the coffee table and stripped. And it was a goddamn good routine, too. She knew what she was doing because in the middle of it she looked at me and asked, "Is it too bright for you?" And then she got down and dimmed the lights and got back up and started dancing to the song again.

I was twenty-six, which means that I had a hard-on if someone attractive breathed heavily across the room. So I could have hit Roger Clemens's fastball with my dick at that point. And after she was done with her routine, she sat on top of me and we had sex on the couch. Then we went to the bedroom and did it again. It was wonderful. Usually when you make love to somebody for the first time, you see the potential but because one of you is a little nervous, it isn't all that it can be. This was spectacular from the beginning.

I essentially moved into her room for the rest of the shoot and after the movie wrapped, we went back to L.A. And that's when I found out that she already had a boyfriend back in England: Hugh Grant. He hadn't done *Four Weddings and a Funeral* yet, and I didn't know who he was—I just figured he was some out-of-work British actor. Little did I know that everyone knew he was going to be a movie star any minute and he was *Vanity Fair* editor Tina Brown's best friend. Once I found out about him, Elizabeth started being honest with me about it. I'd be at her place and she'd say, "Hugh is coming in nine days; when do you think you should start taking your things out?" I'd get tearful and not let her see it. I just loved her. I didn't see other girls, didn't talk about other girls—I was completely enraptured and in her world. But then Hugh would come to town and I'd say to my friends, "I'm done, I don't have to deal with this, I can go out with this other girl who likes me," but I could never do it. I'd make dates with people when he was there, but I never kept them.

It hurts me to say this because she was never really mine, but in many ways Elizabeth was the seminal relationship of my young adulthood. She taught me a lot about myself. She taught me that I wasn't who I thought I was. I'd always thought I was the kind of person who'd never take that kind of treatment from a girl, and what I learned is that I'll take a lot of things from a girl if I love her, and in fact I'll take too much. I really lost myself in Elizabeth Hurley. I didn't do what was best for me. I blew off an audition once just to drive her to the airport when she didn't have a ride.

Eventually I was able to get out of my relationship with Elizabeth but I never really got over her—I just moved on out of emotional necessity. I even ended up dating a friend of hers years later—a British socialite named Linda Evans who lived in the same house with Elizabeth, where all these young actor guys would hang out: people like Gary Oldman and Robert Downey Jr. and a boxer and model named Gary Stretch.

The last time Elizabeth and I saw each other romantically was heartbreaking; I called her up and said, "I can't do this anymore." We went to walk her dog, right after Hugh had left town for the thirteenth time in the three years we were together. I was sitting in her car afterward and I just started crying and she said, "Don't cry. Let's walk the dog." She didn't like tears—no Brits do. They've been bombed by the Nazis: they're tough motherfuckers. She said, "Tom, I'm begging you, please, stop it—I feel bad enough."

She never meant to hurt me; it was just one of those situations. You have to be very mature and sophisticated when handling the intricacies of two people and you throw in a third person; throw in the word *love,* too, and it can be very complicated for somebody who's the object of affection for two different men. And I have to say, Hugh Grant is a wonderful guy. He's truly gifted and also a kind, soft-spoken, humble man. I always liked him, but I've grown to love him for the way he's taken on the wiretapping situation in England. He's a guy who does the right thing. Except, of course, in the case of Divine Brown. And look, I get it: he likes having his cock sucked by different people. So do I. He just should have done it at home. But my point is that in the end, Elizabeth's loyalty was to Hugh.

AT THIS POINT in time, I was making a lot of new friends—mostly actors who seemed to have exciting lives.

One night, not long after I'd been cast in the movie *Heart and Souls,* with Robert Downey Jr., Robert invited me to a party. It got pretty late and a group of us—Robert and five or six girls—ended up in the private music room of his apartment; there was a guitar and piano and a few other instruments. I remember that Robert took out a plastic bag filled with coke and put a whole bunch of it onto this gold plate he had. He was dividing it into lines and I was just watching; the whole thing made me really nervous—especially when everyone started doing the lines. Still, I wanted to be in that room, and everyone else was doing it, and I felt all this pressure—it was all in my head, of course, because I'm sure I could have not done it and no one would have even noticed. But I wanted to be like they were, fabulous or whatever it was in my head that I thought they were. And really, I had no idea at that point that I'd ever end up being an addict. At that point, I never thought I drank alcoholically. The girls went first with the coke and then Robert did it; he passed the straw to me and I thought, "Well, since he did it, then I'm going to."

I'd watched everyone really closely, so it wasn't hard to act like I was familiar with the process. So I just did it: I snorted a line. Nothing happened for a minute or two, and then all of a sudden I felt this incredible rush. It wasn't like a landslide or a tidal wave—instead it was a slow build. Then, undeniably, I felt invigorated and it made the hair on the back of my neck stand up. It felt like Christmas, my birthday, and losing my virginity all at once: everything that was good in my head went off at the same time. I probably should have known right then how much trouble drugs would cause me. I know a lot of people who try coke and say, "Oh it hurts, it burns, I can't sleep." My body's response was the complete opposite of that. I thought, "Wow, this is the greatest thing there is." I remember squeezing my hands together and just getting really quiet as I exhaled. I didn't want anyone to observe me; I just wanted to luxuriate in how I felt.

And then, suddenly, I started to talk—more than I ever had before. I don't even remember what I was saying. But within five minutes, I had done my second line and also pulled Robert aside and said, "Where do you get this stuff?" I was trying to act like I knew what I was talking about, even though I'd literally never been around cocaine before in my life—I think I even said something ridiculous like "Hey, it's pretty bomb dope," thinking that made me sound like some sort of a cocaine veteran. He later told me, when I explained that it had been my first time, that I did a very good job of fooling him.

I ended up staying the night. The next afternoon, he gave me the name and number of the dealer. The guy's name was Gil; I ended up calling him Guilt because that's what I would feel as the years went on and I kept buying coke from him. Robert said to me at the time, "I'm going to give you his number but don't call him until I call you and tell you I've heard back from him—that's the protocol with a drug dealer that doesn't know you." But I couldn't wait.

Within two weeks of doing cocaine, I was a daily cocaine user. It wasn't a sexual thing at first: initially it just left me with a really good feeling, a euphoric kind of confidence. And gradually and then suddenly—like most things in life—my cocaine use evolved into a sexual thing. I'd say after a month, I used it as an aphrodisiac. In the end, all the drugs I ended up doing—except for heroin—I used as aphrodisiacs.

In the back of my head I knew that getting hooked on cocaine wasn't a good idea, but the attitude about drugs was different then, and besides, it felt liberating. I was becoming an actor—and even, in some ways, a star—and this seemed to go with it. I'd always had excessive appetites.

Another thing that thrilled me back then was that I was suddenly mingling with the literary community. I'd always been a big reader, and now I was hanging around with these people. Willem Dafoe and his wife were plugged into that whole world. When I read this book called *Monkeys,* by Susan Minot, it was so beautiful and the author looked so pretty from the picture on it that when Willem told me she was coming to a fund-raiser for his theater, the Wooster Group, I asked if I could come, too. I talked to her for a few minutes that night and stammered the whole time. Willem jokes about it to this day. "You handled it really well with Susan," he'll say. "She thinks you have a learning disability."

I also knew Jay McInerney and Bret Easton Ellis. Downey introduced us at a restaurant in New York's Noho neighborhood, but I'd actually waited on Jay when I was working for Great Performances. Bret was really the wizard of the whole group, but he was so fucked-up you could never talk to him. Even if I hadn't seen him in a year, he'd walk right up to me and ask, "Tom, do you have any more speed?" or "Hi, Tom, I'm out of black." I'd ask, "What's black?" And he'd say, "Heroin." He acted like we'd been doing drugs together forever, and I'd just met him. It was hard to do drugs with Bret because he took all of them: he would steal dope from you when he himself already had dope and a million dollars. It was a trip. I was in a bathroom with him once when I had a bindle of coke, and when I turned around, it was gone. He was the only person there, so I asked him, "Where the fuck's my coke?" And he said, "You're tripping, man, I don't know what you're talking about." And he wouldn't give it back! I hounded him for over an hour and he just said, "Tom, you've lost your mind. You're seeing things and making things up that aren't true. You might want to cut back on the coke."

I was mostly in L.A. at that point, and though Edie and I had broken up, we were still very good friends. That December—the Christmas season of 1992—I went back to New York before going to visit my family in Detroit. When I got to New York, I went to a party with Willem, Edie, and her new boyfriend, Peter Greene—whom she'd met on a movie they did together called *Laws of Gravity*—at Julian Schnabel's. I'd become friendly with Schnabel when I lived in New York in the late 1980s.

Like I said, I was doing a lot of cocaine then, and even though Edie didn't do it, Peter did. He and I had never met before but we became fast friends that night—cocaine has a way of doing that. As the night went on, though, I kept saying to Peter, "We have to get some booze because I don't have any pills or anything to come down with." It was getting toward 4 A.M., when the liquor stores would close, but he kept saying, "Don't worry, I've got something," and I had no idea what it was he had. I said, "Motherfucker, I'm worried about it," because at that point I had started to have paranoid episodes when I was crashing on coke, so I always needed a lot of booze to take the edge off. Edie, Peter, and I finally got in a cab but when the cabbie dropped us off on Perry and Hudson, it was 4:04 A.M. and the liquor store was closed. I threw a major fit but again Peter told me I had nothing to worry about. We went over to Edie's place, which was on Eleventh and Hudson Streets, just four blocks from my apartment, and that's when Peter took me into the bathroom.

He asked me, "Have you ever done heroin before?" I said no but told him that I'd been curious about it. Still, I explained, I didn't want to shoot it. He said that was fine—I could just snort it—and he gave me some China white, a very pure form of heroin. Within a minute of doing it, I knew that it was the best high I'd ever experienced in my life. The coke high was completely obliterated—it was a distant memory. This was every bit of the euphoria I got from cocaine, multiplied by about a million, with absolutely no paranoia, along with this very calm, beautiful feeling that everything was simply perfect. I just lay back on the futon, feeling like I was in heaven for a long time. Eventually I fell asleep and the next afternoon, when we were all pulling ourselves out of bed, I knew that what I'd experienced the night before was something I needed to experience again, as soon as possible, so I asked Peter where he got heroin. He took me down to Alphabet City and explained the process. You walked up to the dealers on the corner of First Street and Avenue A and said, "Hey, what's up?" One of them would ask, "Uptown or downtown?" Uptown was coke and crack; downtown was heroin. It worked. We walked up to them, I said, "Downtown," and the guy took me into a brownstone and sold me heroin.

But it was hard to buy a lot in those days; the dealers just didn't have a lot on them. Peter had to take me to three different spots so that I could get two hundred dollars' worth. And I needed at least that much because I was pretty much a full-blown heroin addict from the beginning.

After a week of doing heroin in New York, I went home to Detroit and kicked at my dad's. It wasn't a horrible withdrawal or anything, since I'd just started doing it, but I'd been doing coke for two and a half months before that, so it wasn't exactly easy, either. I was actually uncomfortable enough to call up this girl that I'd started seeing in L.A. and ask her to come and bring me some coke. She got on a plane that night with four grams of coke stored in a condom in her pussy. She'd never done anything like that before, and I was very grateful. And let's just say that I made a very miraculous recovery from what my mom believed was a bad case of the flu.

My dad, though, knew what was up. (Even though my parents weren't together, my dad was over there a lot.) At one point during that trip I got up in the morning, having not slept at all because I'd been up all night getting high. I was trying to act like it was a normal morning and had been a normal night, that I'd slept the whole time, and he said, "You're certainly going to a lot of trouble to convince someone that you slept. I'm not dumb, Thomas." I asked him what he meant and he walked to my bedroom, where the bed had, of course, not been slept in. He got in it and messed it up and said, "You forgot that beat."

When I got back to L.A. after Christmas, things started to get weird. On the one hand, it felt like I was on this magic carpet ride—that I was young and my life was really happening and this was how I was supposed to feel—but then, very quickly, drugs consumed me, and I'd be locked in my house doing them.

Whenever I'd do coke, if there were people around I'd have to excuse myself and immediately go lock myself in a bathroom in my house once I was high. I'd turn the shower on and act like I was taking a shower for two days. I'm not joking. I'd literally lock myself in there and write a note that would say, "Please leave me alone," thinking that was a really good idea. And for about twenty minutes, I'd think, "I'm so clever—I'm locked in here," but then I'd be scratching and thirsting and losing my mind and thinking zombies were coming out of the walls. People think cocaine makes you the life of the party, and I guess it does at first, but very quickly it made me so paranoid and panicked that I really couldn't talk to people, out of fear of how much they were judging me. So I'd create situations where I could be alone and then I'd end up overwhelmed with loneliness and the desire for company. It was the ultimate catch-22, and there was no solution. I truly don't know how people do cocaine.

With heroin, it was completely different. The high didn't make me paranoid at all. I became a very high-functioning addict, which I actually don't think is as rare as some might think. A lot of drunks and drug addicts do some of their best work while under the influence. That was true even for a heroin addict like Kurt Cobain. The way I started to look at it was this: if I could work sixteen hours a day on a movie set and be really spot-on with my work, then I could do whatever I wanted. Drugs hadn't begun to interfere with how I looked or how I behaved or my work so I didn't see it as a problem. Later, when I realized that I had to do heroin or else I'd get sick, I knew that I had a big problem that I was going to have to deal with, and I was dreading doing that.

Still, in many ways drugs didn't agree with me right from the very beginning, and I was already starting to cancel appointments. I might have been highly functioning, but I was also moving things around and just doing unprofessional things I'd never done before. When I first started acting professionally, if I was told I had to be at an airport at seven thirty in the morning—like I was with *Born on the Fourth of July* and *Lock Up*—that's what I did. I didn't call my agent and say, "Call these motherfuckers up and tell them I'm not going to the airport until three thirty this afternoon; I don't give a fuck what they've got to do or if they have to get me a stork to bring me back." But that was my on-drugs behavior. I'd be partying all night and wouldn't have packed. My place would be a disaster, too, because it had probably been an epic blowout. So I'd try to make all the travel arrangements work around that.

Back then I was getting my drugs from a variety of dealers, but one night, at a big party in the hills, I found the best one of all: Bob Forrest, a guy who'd been the lead singer in the band Thelonious Monster but was now mostly selling drugs. He didn't call himself a drug dealer—he considered himself someone who connected the people who wanted drugs with the drug dealers, but really, what's the difference? He'd been a big musician and a crazy one, too—a guy who would shoot drugs onstage and was best friends with Anthony Kiedis and Johnny Depp. There was a whole scene that Bob was a part of:

John Cusack and Christian Slater and River Phoenix and Leonardo DiCaprio were all a part of it. Bob used to say that musicians always hated actors because actors got paid so much more to do so much less, but that this was a bizarre time when musicians and certain actors were all hanging out and appreciating each other. You'd see Robert Downey Jr. hanging around with Scott Weiland and Bob and Anthony with Johnny Depp.

That first night I met Bob, I had run into Downey and asked him for some coke. He said, "Sizemore, I'm so tired of giving you drugs." I said, "Robert, you make ten million dollars a movie," and he said something crazy because when he was high, he was nuts. I think he said, "Size it up, size it down, get your own, you fucking clown." That pissed me off, so I blew a gram of coke out of the packet he had in his hand.

Then I went downstairs and found the girl throwing the party and asked her if she knew anyone I could buy coke from. She pointed to the corner of the room and said, "Yeah, see that guy with the red hair?" I saw she was pointing at Bob so I said, "That's the guy from Thelonious Monster. He sells drugs?" And she said, "He doesn't just sell drugs; he *is* drugs."

So I walked over to him and asked him if I could get some dope and he said, "Dude, not on the phone, and not here!" He was wearing that fucking hat he always wears, so I knocked it off his head, stepped on it, and said, "Dude! Hatless, on the phone, *and* here!" He just started to walk away without his hat so I grabbed him by the arm and said, "Don't you want your hat?" He actually said, "Unhand me." I said, "What are you, in *Gone with the Wind*?" Then one of his cronies stepped forward—it might have been John Frusciante from the Red Hot Chili Peppers—and I "unhanded" him.

He wasn't really pissed-off—he was just really high. Bob was always really high in those days. He would wake up and smoke four-dollar rocks of crack before he'd even pissed. Anyway, I apologized, told him I wanted to buy in bulk, and asked him to meet me at Duke's Coffee Shop the next day at three thirty with $2,500 worth of coke. He said, "Done."

From there, he became my regular dealer and friend. And I think I was allowed into his circle—actually, he *told* me I was allowed into his circle—because of my appetite for destruction and my talent. This circle wasn't about fame. Keanu Reeves wasn't a part of it. Tom Cruise wasn't there, either. It was a group of people who all sort of felt like rock stars even if they weren't rock stars—people who liked to party and could handle their shit. Kurt Cobain and Courtney Love were in it. It was a group of people who weren't going to snitch on each other. In 1992 and 1993, the whole scene really took place between six or eight houses and a handful of bars, including the Viper Room and Small's K.O., which was on Melrose and Gower and later became Forty Deuce. People wouldn't even really go to Small's—well, you'd go to the bar to see who was there but then you'd end up at this room across the street, doing drugs all night.

Bob would get heroin and coke and drop it off for you at your house. He was a fan of mine, and I was a fan of his, but mostly we were both just fans of drugs. He told me that he and Anthony had this thing where they could look into someone's eyes and immediately know if they were a junkie just like you and you could trust them for life. I think I was a part of that.

I didn't have a lot of perspective on my life then so I never sat back and said, "Hey, I'm a part of this crowd of hot young actors and musicians." I basically just took it for granted that I deserved to be there. I had this weird belief in myself. I didn't think anyone I met was a better actor than I was. I felt like I belonged. Later, when I met Jack Nicholson and Robert De Niro, that felt like a big deal. But I didn't give a shit about actors my age. It was cool to be with those people but I just felt it was where I was supposed to be. And I didn't think of what we were doing as particularly dangerous, really. When River died—and later, when Kurt Cobain died—I was shocked and it broke my heart, but it didn't stop me from doing what I was doing.

Still, I didn't hang out with *anyone* all that much. I was never the guy that hung out. I'd pop into places that were hip and cool, usually just to see if I could meet a girl maybe, but I didn't really spend a lot of time with other guys much at all. I was not ubiquitous on the scene, like some other actors. I liked acting, I liked reading, I liked movies. And I always loved the company of girls. Really, I'm pretty much the same guy today, just without the drugs.

I liked hanging out with Bob Forrest, though—maybe because his addiction back then made mine look minor. He had his own house when I first met him, but he quickly lost it and moved in with Johnny Depp. He'd be driving around in Johnny's cars sometimes and then other people's cars other times. You never really knew if he was supposed to be driving the car he was in. You'd ask him, "Is this car reported as stolen?" And he'd say, "You know, I honestly don't know."

I remember threatening Bob one time; the details are a little murky, but I think I believed he'd stolen one of Johnny's cars and sold it to a chop shop. Even though I had plenty of money, I was always looking for ways to get free dope, so I decided to threaten him by telling him that I'd tell Johnny he stole the car unless he gave me free drugs.

I broke a beer bottle and said, "You see this? I'm going to drive this through your fucking forehead." But he called for Johnny, and I had to get rid of it really fast. As he was helping me clean it up, Bob said, "Even if it was true, who would he believe: hot-tempered Tom or the even-keeled Bob?" I never ended up telling Johnny, and I doubt there was anything to tell. To this day, Bob maintains that he never stole any of Johnny's cars.

He did at one point borrow his girlfriend Stacey Grenrock's car and sell the stereo for drugs. She worked for Johnny at the Viper Room, and Bob was always borrowing her car and then disappearing in it for a few days to do drugs. Eventually Bob was arrested, and everyone decided that they'd had it with bailing him out of trouble. When Bob called Johnny, his assistant—the ex-girlfriend whose car stereo he'd swapped for drugs—wouldn't put the call through and when he tried to call Anthony Kiedis, the Chili Peppers manager also shut him down. He ended up getting sober in jail.

I was really fond of Bob, but he'd been to rehab numerous times already and made many attempts to stay clean, and he just didn't seem to be able to do it. I was nowhere near as fucked-up as he was— which made me think I was okay. I was getting progressively worse, of course, but gradually, whereas Bob was already deeply enmeshed in addiction when I met him.

I think he did nine months in county jail, and when he got out and was clean, he got a job washing dishes at this breakfast place in Silverlake called Millie's. We all felt so bad for him—it was this very hip place so everyone would go there for pancakes and see Bob making minimum wage.

One time John Frusciante actually said to Bob, "I will pay you whatever you make here if you just quit"—but Bob seemed happy. He told me later that the more it weirded people out to see him in that position, the more certain he became that it was the right thing for him to be doing. He started going to AA meetings over at the Gay and Lesbian Center because it was near Millie's and no one would hassle him there or say, "Hey, weren't you once a big-time musician and now

you wash dishes?" We were all so spoiled, but it's like he learned how
to unspoil himself. From there he became an incredible inspiration
to others struggling with addiction. Believe me, if you'd seen the way
Bob did drugs, it would blow your mind that he could be sober for
five minutes, let alone for five days or a year. I don't know if Robert
Downey Jr. or I would have ever gotten sober if we hadn't been able to
say, "My God, if Bob Forrest can get clean, then anyone can." But I'm
getting ahead of myself. My point is that he has helped a whole lot of
people. John Frusciante ended up becoming terribly addicted later:
he had a big black hole in his arm and was pushing a shopping cart
around when Bob found him. Bob took him to Las Encinas, and he
got better. Still, when Bob went to jail we all thought he was the worst
drug addict we'd ever seen. We didn't have any way of knowing then
that I was going to make what he'd been through look minor.

WHEN I GOT called in for *True Romance,* the director Tony Scott talked to
me about playing the role of the assassin who beats up Patricia Arquette.
But I didn't want to beat Patricia Arquette up and then die. I wanted
to play Cody Nicholson—Nickels—to Chris Penn's Nicky Dimes. They
ended up casting my old chess pal Jimmy Gandolfini as the assassin.

Years later, I met with David Chase when he was putting together
The Sopranos. It was just a pilot at that point, but it was awfully good.
Still, I thought back then that TV was beneath me; plus, I'd gained
forty-eight pounds to play John Gotti in a movie and I would have had
to keep the weight on. You never know what's going to turn into the
pop sensation of the decade.

True Romance was only a week of work, but I couldn't believe I was
part of the most amazing cast I'd ever heard of: Christopher Walken

and Gary Oldman and Brad Pitt and Dennis Hopper and Val Kilmer and Samuel Jackson. All my scenes were with Chris Penn, God rest his soul, so we got to know each other really well. His brother Sean came to the set one day and watched us work and we became good friends, too.

We filmed at the abandoned Ambassador Hotel in L.A., where Robert Kennedy was shot, and everyone called that scene "the clusterfuck." Tony started every take like this: "Rock and roll, motherfuckers! Action!" The fucking feathers from the exploding pillows were there for four days. I got killed in one take and had to lie there the whole time with feathers in my mouth.

It was tough keeping a straight face during the scenes with Bronson Pinchot, who had the listening device in his crotch; the laughs in that scene are completely authentic. The part where we're listening to what's going on in the elevator was all improvised. Chris Penn was a wonderful, underrated actor—a real pro.

We did takes where Chris slapped Bronson across the face with the bag of coke, then grabbed him and smashed his head on the table. There'd be some woman talking about her boobs, and all of a sudden Chris Penn would be strangling Bronson. I just about died laughing.

Chris told me, "Sean thinks you're a really good actor, and my brother is the greatest actor in the world." He always used to say that Sean was the greatest actor in the world. It breaks my heart thinking about that because Chris really idolized his brother, and he was just the sweetest guy—a wonderful, funny, talented man lost far too soon.

ALONG WITH MY increase in film opportunities came an increase in drug use and along with that came an increased interest in sex. I had once been a guy who'd assumed he'd stay with one woman his entire life.

But suddenly I was a successful young actor, and it began to dawn on me that my sexual possibilities had opened up exponentially. While of course it was exciting—I knew it was every guy's dream to have this happen—in retrospect I'd say the sex screwed me up almost as much as the drugs. I became addicted to the conquest. I'd meet or find out about a woman and want to know that I could get her. And then I would. I didn't succeed every time, of course, but I succeeded a lot. Obviously it was an ego game. But it wasn't as obvious—at least to me at the time—that it was a sort of Pandora's box I couldn't seem to shut.

The opportunities I would get would blow my mind. In 1989, I got a call from the assistant to a big shot in the industry—literally the biggest star in the world at the time—and was told, "She wants to meet you." When I got there, another of her assistants said, "She'd like you to come this way now," and I was brought into an anteroom. And then this superstar walked in, sat down, and said, "So tell me about yourself."

I said, "Um . . . I'm old enough." I knew what it was all about. We talked for a few more minutes and then she walked out and the assistant came in a minute later and led me up to her room to take a shower. She had probably said, "Have him washed and cleaned" or something, so I took a shower and got into a tub. I was in great shape then, and by the time I actually got into her bedroom, I wasn't nervous at all, even though part of me was thinking, "You're the biggest fucking female star that ever lived—you're a shot-caller. What the hell are you doing here with me?" But I ended up sleeping with her for three years, so I got over that after a while. She liked me. She told me, "You always come through." I think she meant sexually.

By this point, I was also sleeping with Linda Evans, this British socialite I'd met through Elizabeth Hurley. Even though I was head over heels for Elizabeth when I first met Linda, I'd always sort of make sexual overtures to Linda, but in a joking way. At some point, once Elizabeth and I had been finished for a long time, Linda made it clear that she was interested and we got very close very fast. We went out to the Hamptons together, where we stayed at Julian Schnabel's place, and I even took her home to meet my parents. She and I partied together, but we also had a very genuine connection. Honestly, drugs were a part of pretty much all my relationships at that time—I didn't really spend time with anyone who didn't do drugs—and I actually think her drug problem back then was worse than mine. She was mercurial, so the ups were very up and the downs were very down, and I think I believed I could save her and she believed she could save me.

We stayed together on and off for years—though I'd often be juggling several other women at the same time. In the later years we were together, we'd try to quit doing drugs but we would never be able to stay off them. At one point we both stayed sober for thirty days, and then she decided to throw us a party to celebrate that fact at the Monkey Bar. Clearly there were some very basic elements of sobriety that we were failing to understand—or at least incorporate into our lives. We both slipped at that party: each of us took the same friend with us into the bathroom to do coke and told him not to tell the other one that we were using again. The whole thing came out the next day.

Linda was seeing another man during part of the time that we were together, an insanely wealthy European gentleman who lived in New York. When she and I got more serious, she called him up to break things off with him—to tell him she'd fallen in love with me—and he didn't take it very well and kept calling her afterward. She would always be so upset after getting off the phone with him that I called him up and said, "Listen, you're upsetting my old lady really bad." I was so pissed-off that I actually flew to New York to talk to him about it, and we ended up getting in a fistfight. I flew back to L.A.—I had only been gone for something like twelve hours—and never told Linda word one about it. But then he called her and exaggerated the entire thing. She went crazy, and I have to admit that what I did was completely wrong. Drugs had completely clouded my judgment and made me much more likely to do irrational things, like fly to New York to get in a fight with my girlfriend's other boyfriend. I should have at the very least told her I was doing it, but I was so in love with her and I was jealous of him because I felt like he had a hold on her that I didn't, mostly by virtue of the fact that he'd known her longer. She went so crazy that she kicked me in the chest, and I went flying across the room.

I had become pretty good friends with Sean Penn by this point, and he was the one I called whenever I got into a jam with a woman, because he was always really good with women. But when Sean got to our place and saw shit flying across the room and the general state she was in, he said, "I'm leaving—you two are crazy." That was, essentially, the end of my relationship with Linda; we stayed together for about another four months but she could never forgive me for what I did.

Despite all of the insanity, we loved each other—we really did. The truth is that my life was insane at that point, so a crazy relationship fit right in.

EVER SINCE *Born on the Fourth of July,* I'd wanted to work with Oliver Stone again. He was ballsy and brilliant and doing things that no one else was. When I found out that he was putting together *Natural Born Killers*, in 1992, I was told that the only part he thought I was right for was Mickey, the lead, and Warner Bros. essentially told him whom he had to cast for that. Originally he'd hired Michael Madsen, but Warner told him that if he cast Brad Pitt, Tom Cruise, Mel Gibson, or Woody Harrelson, the budget would grow from $7 million to $35 million. Only Mel and Woody read for the part, and Woody was coming off of *White Men Can't Jump* and *Indecent Proposal,* so he was cast. My name never entered the discussion.

But I knew the casting director on *Natural Born Killers;* she called and told me that Oliver was significantly expanding the part of Detective Jack Scagnetti. Still, she said he was leaning toward Gary Oldman or Jimmy Woods. I knew the entire Mickey monologue by heart, so one night at the Monkey Bar, when I saw Oliver there I went up to him and said, "I can't believe you're going to cast Woody as Mickey." And I started in on Mickey's monologue right then and there. This is obviously a profoundly bad idea in a lot of ways, but I was doing it well, I guess, and I actually followed him out to his car to finish it. When I was done, he looked at me and said, "You know what? Come to my office tomorrow. I want to hear that monologue again and put you on tape doing it." So I went to his office the next day and did it again. When I was done this time, he said, "What do you think about playing Scagnetti?" I was still very focused on somehow getting the part of Mickey, so I said I didn't know. He was leaving his office for the day and he said, "Walk with me to my car." We started walking to his car and he said, "Walk like Scagnetti would walk," so I started doing that. Then he asked, "Do you think Scagnetti would have change in his pocket?" He induced me into the character like that. Then he had me follow him in my car to his house in Malibu, and we worked on the character of Scagnetti for a couple of hours.

When my agent called to tell me that I'd officially gotten the part, I was high on coke and on my way to get more. But when I heard that the movie was starting in a little less than three months, I called the dealer back right away and canceled the transaction. I just thought, "How am I going to do a lead role in an Oliver Stone movie in eighty-seven days if I'm fucked-up?"

I didn't really know how to get sober, so I called Bobby Pastorelli, an actor I'd met on a movie I'd done called *Striking Distance*. He played the house painter in *Murphy Brown* and later OD'd—I think he might have killed himself—but at the time he was in AA and he started taking me to meetings.

My agents and the people I worked with didn't really know I'd been doing drugs and I was hoping I could get off them before the movie started. I wasn't a dummy; I knew that the club of actors who get opportunities like the one I was about to get was small, and I didn't want to fuck it up.

I actually managed to put together nearly three months of clean time before the movie started. And before the table read, I had a private meeting with Oliver where he said, "I'm building a table, okay? And I've got Robert Downey Jr. and Juliette Lewis and Tommy Lee Jones and Woody Harrelson. I've got four good legs already. Do you get what I mean?" And I just said, "I promise you, I'm not going to fuck up your table."

We started working in L.A., at Hollywood Center Studios, and then we flew out to Winslow, Arizona, for the shoot. Oliver and I were closer by then. He loved that I knew so many Shakespeare monologues—he'd come to my room, in his footsie pajamas, and say, "Come on, Tom, do that monologue again." It was hilarious.

Playing Scagnetti was a defining moment for me. In the beginning, I couldn't identify with him, really—with his viciousness and his pettiness. I had to steep myself in serial murder. I read Bundy interviews. I met serial killer John Wayne Gacy on death row in Illinois. I made myself sick. I felt sick, like there was a tumor in me. Even in the hair: I had an *Eraserhead* haircut. I lost twenty-two pounds so that I could turn myself into a snake—a lizard and cold-blooded killer with no remorse or conscience. I got very heavily into the character but I sort of cut myself off from normal society in the process.

The hysteria when the movie came out was kind of ridiculous. Obviously Oliver makes controversial movies, but John Grisham went out and said that Oliver should be held accountable for the fact that two kids who watched the movie killed someone; that was simply an ignorant thing to say. The movie was meant to alarm. It wasn't meant to enrage young people to go out and kill people—that wasn't what Oliver Stone was saying. He was saying that in twentieth-century America there's a premium on the media, violence, and fame, which can lead to enshrinement in a virtual hall of fame for misdeeds.

Very early in the shoot I had to do a scene where I strangle a naked girl and orgasm in the process, and I was incredibly nervous—I think because so much of what goes on in that scene just isn't right. It was one of the girl's first acting roles, and she was nervous as hell, and that didn't help. We did two takes and Oliver came up and said to me, "Come on, take a break for a minute and think about what you're doing." I panicked. I just couldn't pull it together, and all I could think was that I'd be more free and easy and with it if I were on some sort of drug. That really was my coping mechanism, even at that early stage.

So I asked someone on the set, "Can you get me a bottle of whisky, and if it's possible—don't tell anybody—but can you get me a gram of coke?" This was a different time. It was 1993 and it was an Oliver Stone set and you could talk fairly freely about most things, although you wouldn't say something like that in front of Oliver.

I'm sure I could have done the scene without drugs; this was really just an excuse for me to use; in retrospect, I realize my addiction was already a monster. Anyway, the guy came back, motioned to the fake coke I was supposed to snort in the scene, and said, "Dump that shit out." Then he said, "Merck, so be cool," as he put the new stuff out. Merck is pharmaceutical pure coke—Keith Richards talks about it in his book. It was really good for a while, but it turned on me fast: it made me really paranoid. In any case, that night I took a couple of swigs and did some real coke and I was able to do that scene with that gal and do it well.

Juliette Lewis had come to the set for her karate lesson because the next day she was going to shoot the scene where she beats the guys up in the diner. I had actually met her originally at the rehearsal and liked her right away. I knew Brad Pitt, her former boyfriend, because we'd played hoops together, so I'd asked him back then if it was okay with him if I went after her. He said, "Is it okay? I'll drive you there! I want to be your agent on this one!" I think she was bothering him—phone calls and stuff. But actually, she was the one who left him, not the other way around. She left him over a pair of shoes, I swear to God. She had been nominated for an Oscar for *Cape Fear*— nobody knew who he was at that point but he was her boyfriend— and I guess he made them late to the Academy Awards because he couldn't decide which pair of shoes to wear. The limo was waiting and she couldn't get him out of the house. She was sixteen and she dumped him over that.

By the time Juliette showed up on the set, I already had a huge crush on her. She was only eighteen years old, and I really believed she was an intuitive genius—her talent was really, really sexy and attractive to me. So she was standing there watching me and when the scene was done, she said something like "Hey, Tom, that was really good. Are you like that with all the girls? I've often wanted to be strangled to death." And she started laughing.

I said, "Yeah, I've strangled several girls to death myself. That's why

My mom was and still is beautiful. She and my dad met when she was 13 and he was 14. (Copyright Judith K. Sizemore)

My dad with Aaron and me. My dad's high school picture literally said "Boy Genius" below it, and he expected the same from his boys. (Copyright Judith K. Sizemore)

With my younger brother Aaron when I was six. We shared a bedroom and when noises would frighten me late at night, he'd try to stay awake until I fell asleep. (Copyright Judith K. Sizemore)

With my grandparents, Blevins and Vina Sizemore. Blevins worked at a machinist shop, but they were still dirt poor. (Copyright Judith K. Sizemore)

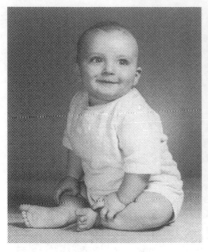

Me as a baby. I was supposedly saying complete sentences by the time I was two and reading by the age of four. (Copyright Judith K. Sizemore and Thomas E. Sizemore, Sr.)

Me and Aaron with our mom, who's holding Paul. This is our last Christmas before my mother, Aaron, Paul and I moved back to Detroit. I was 16 and in 11th grade. (Copyright Thomas E. Sizemore, Sr.)

Kissing my mom's mom, Grandmother Mildred Schannault, at my wedding. When my mom was growing up, Grandma and my Grandpa Schannault made their house into an after-hours joint to earn extra money. (Copyright Judith K. Sizemore)

With Bruce Willis, my costar in *Striking Distance*. This was also the movie where I met Robert Pastorelli, who ended up taking me to my first AA meeting. (Copyright Tom Sizemore)

With Robert De Niro, my dad and Maeve on the set of *Heat*. My dad asked De Niro to take care of me and De Niro laughed and said he would try. (Copyright Aaron Sizemore)

With Michael Rappaport (third from left), Edie Falco (fourth from left), and some friends. Michael and I met on *True Romance*. It was only a week of work but starred some of the greats: everyone from Christopher Walken and Dennis Hopper to Samuel Jackson, Brad Pitt, Val Kilmer and Gary Oldman. (Copyright Tom Sizemore)

Me and my dad with Gary Oldman and his kids. (Copyright Tom Sizemore)

Me with actor Michael Wincott (on the right) and another friend. We worked together early in my career, on *Born on the Fourth of July* and *Strange Days*. (Copyright Tom Sizemore)

On *Devil in a Blue Dress*. That was a terrific movie I made in between *Natural Born Killers* and *Strange Days*. (Copyright Tom Sizemore)

Me playing Scrooge in a Wayne State University production of *A Christmas Carol*. My little brother Paul played Tiny Tim. Wayne State was where I first started to get positive feedback about my acting. (Copyright Tom Sizemore)

On the set of *Flight of the Intruder* with my costar Brad Johnson, the director John Milius and my former manager Suzan Bymel. (Copyright Tom Sizemore)

On the set of *Hustle*, the Pete Rose movie, which was directed by the great Peter Bogdanovich. Peter told me he didn't worry about people's reputations because John Ford's wife had told him, "If you want to stay in the movie business, never believe everything you hear and only believe half of what you see." (Copyright Tom Sizemore)

On the set of *Red Planet* with Simon Baker, during an all-too-rare moment when everything wasn't going awry. Val Kilmer and I actually came to blows on the set after he threw a lit cigarette at a prop girl. (Copyright Tom Sizemore)

On the set of *Robbery Homicide Division*. I was working with my *Heat* director, Michael Mann, and doing some of the best work of my career, but my life was on the verge of falling apart. (Copyright Tom Sizemore)

On the set of *Black Hawk Down* with William Fichtner. I stayed sober on the set by playing a lot of chess with Ewan McGregor; I think he beat me 664 games in a row. (Copyright Tom Sizemore)

On the set of *Flight of the Intruder*. Willem Dafoe, whom I'd met on *Born on the Fourth of July*, was in it, as was Rosanna Arquette—someone Edie Falco and I thought of as the epitome of a famous actress when we were struggling. (Copyright Tom Sizemore)

My twin sons, Jayden and Jagger. If they misbehave, I give them a "time out" but I try to tell them, "I don't approve, but I love you." (Copyright Tom Sizemore)

On the set of *Strange Days*. It was my second time working with Juliette Lewis while we were involved. The shoot took 17 weeks. (Copyright Tom Sizemore)

Me photographed by Sean Penn. Sean was the guy I always called whenever I got into a jam with a woman because he's really good with women. (Copyright Sean Penn)

On the set of *Saving Private Ryan* with my dad and stepmom. My dad didn't come to a lot of my movie sets but he flew to Wexford Island for this one. Maeve and I were patching things up again and she spent a lot of time on the set as well. (Copyright Tom Sizemore)

I was so good; it was easy to do. So whenever you want to be strangled to death, you know who to call." She said, "I'd like to be strangled to death right now." That was how we flirted with each other.

Later, she left a message at my hotel room, and that night we used heroin together and had sex. Once I started using heroin again, it was like I'd never stopped and my eighty-seven days of sobriety were a distant memory. Heroin just put this hazy gauze over everything and made Juliette seem even more glamorous than she already seemed to me at the time as a two-time Oscar nominee. But what we did together was anything but glamorous. We were at the Best Western—the only hotel in Winslow—getting high and ordering corn flakes. We ordered like twenty-nine bowls of that shit. We could never eat it all—we were too high or it made us sick—so it would sit there, and we'd order some more, and that would get soggy.

During the shoot, when we had breaks, Juliette and I would come back to L.A. to get more dope. I was just snorting and smoking, not shooting, and I wasn't feeling too bad about it, either, because I felt like I was doing great work. Of course I was addicted again, but when I was working I used the minimal amount of dope, just enough not to get sick from withdrawal. I'd use enough to get what heroin addicts call "well"—which really just meant to get normal. Basically, if I was using sixty dollars' worth of smack during the breaks, then I'd use ten to fifteen dollars' worth a day once I was back on set—so little that I wouldn't even be noticeably impaired. If I felt sickness coming on again, I'd do a little bit more. I never wanted to be high—or at least be seen as high—on a movie. People really didn't know that I was using, but they did eventually become suspicious because I was with Juliette all the time, and she briefly became inoperative; she couldn't stay awake during the takes.

Her agents flew out and everyone asked me what was going on.

I told them, "I don't know what she's doing. I just fuck her and I go back to my room. Whatever she's doing, she's doing when I'm asleep." They sort of believed me, even though my own problem wasn't exactly under control. I was doing a lot of running around and juggling.

Some of that juggling involved the fact that I'd met someone else. See, one day, when we were shooting the courtroom scene where Juliette is testifying, I saw what had to be the prettiest extra in the history of extras: she had blond hair, beautiful teeth, and an unbelievable body. Her name was Maeve Quinlan. I was standing next to Woody Harrelson when I saw her, and he said, "Who's gonna fuck her first?" We started taking bets. I said, "Robert," talking about Downey. He said, "I bet it's you or me—or maybe Oliver. How about I go second and you go third?" And I said, "I don't care when I go, as long as I get a chance." I didn't know then that I was talking about my future wife.

Maeve was actually Juliette's stand-in and they just happened to use her as an extra on that courtroom day. She and Juliette didn't look anything alike, but they were both petite, and with a brunette wig on, Maeve could stand in for her.

When the scene wrapped, Maeve was walking down the courthouse steps in front of me, and I just busted out with "You have the greatest ass I think I have ever, ever seen." She turned around and said, "And you have the most pathetic come-on line I have ever, ever heard. Does that line actually work?" As she kept walking down the courtroom steps, I burst into laughter. I couldn't believe how brazenly she'd just called me out on my shit. Then she turned around and started laughing as well, and it was one of the most beautiful sights I'd ever seen. I said to her, "Oh shit, now you've really done it. Great ass, great grin. What's next—great heart?" She just kept laughing, and I know this sounds ridiculous but as we stood there, laughing and looking at each other, it's like everything went into soft focus.

The truth is, the whole time I knew Maeve—and that goes up through today—her ass, her grin, and her heart were and are pretty much the best I've ever come across. What I didn't know that day but I would soon come to find out is that she was completely unlike any other girl I'd ever met: she came from this amazing family in Chicago, had graduated from the University of Southern California on a full-ride tennis scholarship, and her dad and brothers were all doctors. You don't ever find girls like her on movie sets; you don't really find girls like her anywhere.

I'd heard that Woody made a run at her and she turned him down, and I think I used that as a reason to talk to her the next time I saw her. I went up to her and said, "I heard my buddy went after you." At first, she denied it to protect him, which really endeared her to me. She could have said something bad, but instead she said it was completely untrue.

One day I asked her if she wanted to have lunch with me. The cast and crew usually ate meals together, but I sometimes liked to eat in my trailer alone, and so when I asked her to eat with me, I meant alone with me there. But when we got our food and I nodded in the direction of my trailer, she just shook her head. It was clear then that with her I wasn't going to be able to get away with the kind of things I could with other women.

What's funny is she had actually seen me before that day at the courthouse and thought I was an idiot. Back when we were all at Hollywood Center Studios—which is where we were working before we went on location to Arizona—she passed me on the lot. Apparently I was standing there in my underwear, with my sunglasses on my forehead, smoking a cigarette. She told me later that she just thought, "Who the hell walks around a public place in underwear acting like he's in jeans? It's one thing to do it in wardrobe and your trailer but in the middle of the lot?" But while she was partially horrified, I think another part of her found it refreshing. Like I said, she'd had this extremely proper upbringing, and I don't think she'd been around many people who didn't really give a fuck about what people thought.

So we became friends during the shoot. She had a boyfriend back in Chicago, and I was really with Juliette, but I knew already that I genuinely liked Maeve a lot. And believe it or not, I had two other women that I was also involved with at the time. One was Vanessa Lasky, a wonderful girl who was the assistant to the manager I was with at the time, Suzan Bymel. When I first signed with Suzan, she had said to me, "Whatever you do, don't get involved with my assistant," and, of course, that was the first thing I did. Vanessa and I were involved for years, on and off; she eventually ended up marrying a CAA agent named Steve Alexander and becoming a successful interior designer.

I was also still seeing the British socialite Linda Evans, and the crazy thing about this particular time in my life is that I wasn't *casually* dating any of these women: I felt like I was passionately in love with Vanessa, Juliette, and, later, with Maeve, too. I do believe it's possible to love more than one woman at a time, but even I knew that this many women was excessive.

When the movie wrapped, Juliette and I came back to L.A., and even though I was sharing my apartment on Harratt with Vanessa, I was spending a lot of time in this $2.5 million house Juliette had bought on Outpost Drive in Hollywood. At one point we even talked about me paying the mortgage with her, but I just could never get it together to move my stuff in from my apartment and neither could she; so she kept a place she had up on Sunset Plaza and I kept the one I had with Vanessa. And ironically, while we had all these places to live, the house we were mostly living in, on Outpost, had no furniture in it.

I went straight from *Natural Born Killers* to *Devil in a Blue Dress* and then I had a little break before *Strange Days*. That's when my managers suggested I go to a rehab program at UCLA. They had a thirty-day program on Santa Monica Boulevard, and I went and stayed for a month—and then got high within four hours of getting out. I thought I wanted to be clean, but I found out I didn't—something I didn't know then would grow to be a pattern. And I just didn't understand the whole concept of staying away from certain people, places, and things. I understood what it meant but it just didn't seem doable then.

And in many ways, heroin really worked for me in those days. I remember every detail of what it was like to go cop when I was back in L.A. after *Natural Born Killers* had wrapped. I remember the way the heroin smelled in my car. I remember that we were still living in the aftermath of the riots so the cops weren't bothering as much with trying to arrest people for drug possession. I would drive downtown, to Bonnie Brae and Third Streets at nine fifteen in the morning, knowing that I'd be able to go home afterward and watch a football game on DirecTV. And I'd feel on top of the world in my fancy car. After copping, I'd stop at a market and buy a moon pie. I'd put a Chet Baker cassette on and damn it if the whole scenario didn't feel romantic to me. I'd be holding the heroin in my hand knowing that if I were stopped, I could just swallow a balloon. But I was never stopped.

Usually I'd pull over and either roll up a dollar bill and snort the heroin or put it on tinfoil and put a lighter under it and smoke it just a few blocks away from where I got it. You couldn't get bad heroin then—heroin then was only bad if you stepped on it. Speed can be bad because it's man-made, but heroin was beautiful, especially in those days. I'd take four hits, then I'd drive down that hill with Chet Baker still playing, and I thought I was just the coolest motherfucker. Or maybe *cool* isn't the right word. I just felt beyond the reach of pain. Above it all. Like I was floating above this horrible morality play called the *Interpersonal Relationships of the Young and Successful and the Mysteries of Young Adulthood*. I'm not kidding about that name, either: if you look back at some of the journals I was keeping then, I'd write that shit down. Before then, I'd felt the first stirrings of loneliness—my first heartbreaks—and I didn't like it at all. Heroin got me above all of it. Heroin allowed me to watch other people trudge the road—ironically, that's a phrase from the AA Big Book, but the truth is I looked at people who were suffering through normal life pain and I thought they were nuts. My guy friends would talk about liking girls and I'd watch them risking getting rejected and getting their feelings hurt and I'd think they were out of their minds for putting up with that stuff.

Strange Days was a really difficult movie. It filmed for seventeen weeks in the summer of 1994, and it went on and on. It was a brilliant film, though, in a lot of ways. James Cameron wrote the script, which was about an ex-cop—played by Ralph Fiennes—who deals disks that contain recorded memories and emotions that people become addicted to. Cameron was originally going to direct it but instead Kathryn Bigelow, who had been married to him and whom I'd worked with on *Point Break*, did. And completely coincidentally—having nothing to do with me—Maeve ended up working as a production assistant on *Strange Days*.

Maeve and I had actually been in touch since *Natural Born Killers* had wrapped, because the whole time I was with Juliette and juggling Vanessa, I was also pursuing her. Our relationship was purely platonic because she still had her boyfriend, and I liked her all the more for the fact that she wouldn't jump into bed with me the way other women would. I would basically call her every morning and ask her out for coffee, and every morning she would say no. But I could tell that she liked me and that I was wearing her down. And then one night she found out that her boyfriend in Chicago had been cheating on her. I didn't know that yet, of course, but the next morning when I called and asked her out for coffee, she said yes. Coffee turned into her coming back to my apartment on Harratt and listening to Sheryl Crow's first album, which I was obsessed with at that point, and that turned into her not leaving for two days. Although she refused to have sex with me, we made out for pretty much forty-eight hours straight, and she slept in my arms—the only woman I'd ever done that with who didn't have sex with me. They were truly the most romantic two days of my life. Of course, our relationship couldn't develop from there because I was still with Vanessa—who, conveniently enough, had been in New York during those two days—and also with Juliette, but Maeve and I remained friends.

At the same time, I thought I was in love with Juliette. In retrospect, I think I was in love with the whole idea of her. And I was in love with what was happening in my career more than anything else. When Juliette and I were up in her house, things got really weird. First off, at age thirty-two, I was significantly older than she was. And even though she had a nascent intelligence and a kind of knowledge about human nature, she'd never gone to college, and she had a very different upbringing from me. So after we got over the lustful part at the beginning, we didn't have a lot in common aside from the fact that we both liked to do a lot of drugs. And she never wanted to leave the house, ever—not even to go outside. We had a big TV with porn playing 24/7, which I thought was cute in the beginning, but it started to wear on me after a while. I'd say, "Turn it off" and she'd say, "But I like the *music*"—which I thought was one of the great lines of all time. Still, whenever I looked up, it seemed like there was some guy's big hairy ass on the screen. At one point, I taped something over the screen for a while, but she took it off.

All we had, furniture-wise, was a huge bed and one end table. It was a weird setup, made weirder by the fact that she didn't want me to leave the room. I'd get up to go take a shower and she'd go, "Where are you going? Can I come with you?" And she'd get a blanket, come into the bathroom, and sleep on the floor and wait for me.

Juliette had been a star since she was fifteen and in some ways she was very mature, but she also had a way of keeping people away from her. She really was a sweetheart; she just didn't understand all the adulation she received. In many ways, I don't think she was comfortable in the spotlight.

At a certain point, for some reason she decided she didn't want to see her brother's face anymore—and that was a problem since he was working as her assistant. So she had me paint this sentence on the outside of the bedroom door: "I don't want to ever see you again, your sister." And then she insisted I get a saw, carve a hole in the bedroom door, and paint "Deliver all food here." We literally didn't leave the room after that and never saw anyone. The food would be brought up, and we'd just stay there. She'd originally wanted her brother to buy furniture for the house, but she never gave him any money because she didn't know what to do with the place. I walked around the house once and told her, "You know, this is a really great house—let's furnish this fucking thing and live in it," and she'd say, "I like this *room*." Essentially, we were really high and really rich.

I was still fairly new to heroin then and honestly, it felt like the best thing about it was going out to score. The euphoric anticipation—the excitement of knowing you were about to be altered, in a profoundly positive way—was the greatest high there was to me back then. Even if I was dope-sick, I loved going to cop because I knew I wasn't going to be sick long.

With heroin, especially back then, you couldn't just buy from one guy: the dealers, like the dealers in New York's Alphabet City, didn't have enough. And dope was different strengths. It sounds insane, I realize, but if you ever heard that a guy OD'd from a certain batch of heroin, you'd find out who his dealer had been because you knew that heroin was good.

Juliette and I would go through phases where we'd try to quit. I know people who decide to quit suddenly and start flushing all their drugs down the toilet, but I never did it like that: I'd make sure I'd do all the drugs and then, when I was done, I'd say, "Okay, I'm not going to do that anymore." I'd make it a day, sometimes two—I'd never make it more than three. By then, my feet would start to get real heavy and I'd go, "Fuck it, I know how to fix this."

Of course, things were getting strange up there on Outpost: when you're doing that many drugs, things have a way of always getting strange. And I was actually starting to get a little worried about Juliette. So one day I asked her brother to call her manager, Joel Stevens, who was a Scientologist and a really nice guy. And one night Joel just barged in there and Juliette picked up the nearest large object she could find and threw it right at his fucking head, hitting him in the face. He was bleeding everywhere, and she was screaming, "Bad, bad, bad idea! Bad idea! Bad idea, Joel! You could have upset Tom!" Like she was worried about me.

That led to an intervention of sorts on her. She'd been to rehab before, and she knew it was coming. She told me she wanted me to say that I wanted to get clean as well so they'd let us go to rehab together.

I asked her, "Will we get clean?"

She said, "No, we'll go to Scientology rehab and we don't have to really get clean there."

Three days later, Juliette's agent, Joel, her mom, her dad, her brother, and some girlfriends came up. I'd heard about interventions—I was only a few months away from my own, but of course I didn't know that at the time. It was tedious. I remember thinking, "I'll never let this happen to me." They carted her off to Narconon, the Scientology rehab—I didn't end up going after all—and that was pretty much the end of our relationship.

While Juliette and I haven't talked since the late 1990s, I hear she's sober now. I know she's somewhat off the map, but I think, knowing her the way I did, that that's a conscious choice. She plays in a band called Juliette and the Licks, and the sense I get is that she didn't want to do movies anymore. I think her early success and all the drugs and getting involved with Brad Pitt and then having him become such a mega star made her feel like the world of being a motion picture star was a hurtful place to be. She always loved music—she wrote and sang a song called "Born Bad" in *Natural Born Killers* and she also sang in *Strange Days*. I think she saw the music world as kinder than the movie one. And who knows—she may be right.

CHAPTER 4

LOSING IT

IN MANY WAYS, once Juliette and I weren't involved anymore, my life started to feel normal again. I was still doing heroin but considerably less than when I was with Juliette, and my agents and managers seemed very positive about the direction my career was headed in. But I had no idea just how well things were going until I got a call one day from my agent at the time, Bryan Lourd.

"Robert De Niro wants to meet you tomorrow night at the Monkey Bar for dinner," he said. Of course I didn't believe it—Robert De Niro had been my idol since I'd first seen *Taxi Driver*, so I thought it was somebody playing a joke on me. I said, "Who is this? This isn't funny." But it was Bryan, and he was serious. Some people think I'm egotistical, but I've always been somewhat insecure about my work, and was especially so back then. I just couldn't believe it.

I had met De Niro before, when I did a movie called *Guilty by Suspicion* in 1991. On that shoot he was all about the work, and I only had two scenes, so we didn't get to know each other too well. But two years later, when I got this call from Bryan, De Niro and Michael Mann were putting together *Heat,* and I guess De Niro had seen *True Romance* and *Natural Born Killers* before their release. He had been interested in Quentin Tarantino—he was thinking about *Jackie Brown* already—and he wanted to see Quentin's work. Quentin had written both *Natural Born Killers* and *True Romance. Natural Born Killers* was actually the first script Quentin sold—Jane Hamsher and Don Murphy bought it from him when he was still working at a video store and selling scripts out of the trunk of his car. Don Murphy told me the story. Don was renting a Japanese movie from the video store where Quentin worked, and they started talking. Quentin said he was a screenwriter and gave him copies of *Natural Born Killers, True Romance,* and *Reservoir Dogs.* Don called up Jane and said, "There's a genius working at the Manhattan Beach video store." And they bought *Natural Born Killers.*

Anyway, De Niro apparently really liked my performances in *True Romance* and *Natural Born Killers* so he asked Michael Mann if he knew of me. Michael didn't, so Bob had the two movies screened for him and said, "It's your choice—you're the director," but he made it clear he wanted me to play Michael Cheritto.

But I didn't know any of this at the time. Once I realized Bryan wasn't joking, I asked him why De Niro wanted to have dinner with me. Bryan said, "I don't know, but I'm sure he'll tell you." I was terrified and told Bryan I didn't want to do it. But I got it together and showed up that night at the Monkey Bar. I was extremely nervous, so I just sat down with De Niro and said, "Before we start, I have to tell you something. I've had a picture of you on my wall since I was fifteen, and I still have it on my wall even though I'm a grown-up, and it's the first thing I see every morning." It was true. It's this huge poster that I bought through a magazine, and I still have it to this day even though it's really torn up.

He said, "What?" And I thought, "I've said the worst thing ever." I felt like a dipshit. So then I said, "I can't believe I'm sitting here, I've been a fan of—oh, fuck it, man." Thinking I'd screwed everything up, I got up to leave. And he just said, "What are you doing? Sit down."

I felt even worse so I just said, "No, I'm going to go" again and he said, "I don't mean to make you feel bad—it's really nice that you're a fan of mine." So I sat back down and asked, "Why am I here? What do you want?"

He said, "If you give me the opportunity to talk, I'll tell you." It was true; I hadn't given him a second. I just said, "Hey, before we start," right away because I was nervous. So then he said, "I saw *True Romance* and *Natural Born Killers*," and I said, "Oh no you didn't," because they hadn't come out yet, and I hadn't even seen them. I wasn't too savvy yet and didn't know that people could screen movies before they come out; I'd never been invited to a screening. He was very patient and found my naïveté charming, I guess. And then he said, "Do you know what a wonderful actor you are?" I wanted to believe him so badly. This was a really seminal day in my life. I mean, I knew I was working a lot and *Natural Born Killers* was a big thing, but other actors were in it, and I hadn't seen the movie yet so I wasn't sure at that point how much I had ended up in it—if my part had been cut significantly. And I really wanted to be a movie star and not just an actor. Not to compare myself to somebody like Kobe Bryant, but my attitude was "I want the ball." I don't trust anyone else, and as an actor I knew what I was going to do: I'm going to take the ball down, muscle it up, and either make the fucking shot or get fouled. It's that moment where you're either going to win the game or not. This was a moment where I thought I might end up winning the game.

And once I met Michael Mann, I was cast in the movie. It was the first time I didn't have to audition for a part—something I'd long dreamed of happening.

To prepare for my role, I spent time at famous Folsom Prison, the maximum-security facility near Sacramento, California. I wanted to gain insights into criminal psychology and felonious "crews" like the fictional one my character was a part of. I said to this one convict when I was there, "Your rap sheet says you killed five people. You wanna talk to me about that?" He responded, "I only killed two people." I said, "Well, it says here five." And he goes, "Oh, those others were cops." He said it in a really nondramatic, flat-toned way. So I pressed him and said, "Well, I don't know how you view them from your world, but I think most people would think that police officers are people—with wives and children and loved ones." He just looked at me blankly and went, "Uh huh."

We first gathered in December 1994 and there was a very lengthy training time for us to get comfortable with the guns—about nine weeks, the majority of which we spent practicing at a gun range out by Magic Mountain. It may have been overkill on Michael's part, but that shoot-out scene would never have been as effective without all that training. In my opinion, it's possibly the best shoot-out scene in the history of movies, and in some ways it's the centerpiece of the movie.

I became good friends with De Niro during the training because I had no experience at all with weapons, and Bob had done *The Deer Hunter* and other movies where he'd used them. People think I'm this gun guy because there have been guns in so many of my movies, but, especially back then, I was afraid of guns; I didn't know how they worked or anything. In *True Romance* I come into a room and say, "Put your gun down," and then get shot. In *Natural Born Killers*, I pull a gun out and get shot by Juliette Lewis. But I hadn't done much gunplay myself until *Heat.* Later of course, on *Saving Private Ryan* and *Black Hawk Down,* I learned how to use weapons even more. In any case, I liked the training because I enjoyed knowing what I was doing in movies, and Bob was very helpful because he could tell I was gun-shy, so to speak.

But at the same time that I was prepping to star in this big movie and becoming close with the man who had essentially made me want to become an actor, I picked up heroin again in a pretty major way. I cut down on using when I initially left Juliette, but then, over-whelmed, I think, by these incredibly exciting things that were hap-pening in my career, I got right back to using large amounts fairly quickly. I just started doing it the same way I had on *Natural Born Kill-ers,* buying just enough to get by when I was working. One of the gun trainers—a guy named Mick Gould—was really helpful. He not only helped me with the weapons but also with confidence. He knew I was struggling with drugs, and he would talk to me about trying to get my body and mind working together. He was a really good guy, and he'd say things like "Let's get your body strong again—let's get these drugs out of your body." But I was addicted and, while I appreciated what he was trying to do, I knew there was no way of getting the drugs out of my body then.

De Niro didn't really know the extent of it and he was really won-derful to me. I learned a lot from him about how to behave. He was never late, he never bitched or complained, and he never pulled any movie star shit. Al Pacino was the same way. They were both just in-credible, sweet people who knew everybody's name on the set.

The shoot, which officially started on March 3, 1995, went eighty-six days over. That was nearly twice as long as it was supposed to be, which was ninety days. I remember on the third day, when Michael Waxman, who was the first assistant director, said, "We're five days behind," I asked him, "How is that possible? It's only day three." And he told me, "We haven't even set up day two's work yet." I looked at the call sheet and saw that half of the call sheet from day one was still on the call sheet of day three. But this wasn't because Michael was irresponsible—it was actually the opposite problem; it was because of the exacting standards of Michael, the director of photography Dante Spinotti, Bob, and Al. All four of those guys were really involved. Bob had directed *A Bronx Tale* by then, and he had plans to direct more, so he would be behind the camera, and you had four guys who had to agree that they had something the way it should look. The studio was getting worried. Bob Daly and Terry Semel, who were running Warner Bros. at the time, would come to the set at least every week because they were worried. But I don't think it could have been done any other way.

Val Kilmer and I became good friends during the shoot even though we argued a lot. We'd argue about the stupidest things, too, like why I laughed at some joke De Niro made about Val playing Batman. We'd get in these fights and act like two girls and say things like "Don't call me again" before stomping out of the room. We hadn't interacted at all on *True Romance* but I'd actually met him on the set of *The Doors* when I was there to see Oliver, and another time years before that, but he didn't remember. When I was still a waiter I saw him do *'Tis Pity She's a Whore* at the Juilliard School in New York and went backstage to meet him. At the time, he was the best young actor I'd ever seen. I told him I was an actor as well, and he looked at me like, "Yeah, sure," and walked away; he had bodyguards already.

We ended up having a falling-out on *Red Planet*, and then we became friends again. Val was very supportive when my life fell apart later, but then he mysteriously disappeared. I've reached out to him numerous times, but he's really inaccessible now.

During the shoot, Val and I would go out at night together, and I remember one time we were at a place called the Formosa. I think I was still mystified by the fact that my fame afforded me the opportunity to get away with all kinds of things with women. Most normal people, if they were going to talk to a girl in a bar, would say something like "How are you doing? My name's Tom. Can I buy you a drink?" or "What's your name?" Or something. But I was just an animal, so I said to this girl, "What's your pussy look like?" And the saddest part isn't that I said it—although that was sad—but that when she walked away, I actually thought she was going to the bathroom to check and see what her pussy looked like so she could come back and tell me.

Val looked at me as she was walking away and said, "Tom, what's wrong with you?"

I went, "Val, she's going to see what it looks like."

He shook his head and said, "She just left the bar, asshole. The bathroom's the other way." And he was right. Of course he was right. What I said was so ludicrous that she didn't even bother saying, "How dare you" or "You're an asshole." If some girl came up to me and asked me what my dick looked like, I'd say, "You've lost your mind, girl, something's wrong with you." Believe me, I never said that to a woman again.

The truth is that I was always awkward around girls, even though girls tended to like me. In many ways, I don't think I learned how to really talk to girls until recently. I said a lot of dumb shit. And I was high pretty much all the time, which made what was happening not feel entirely real and also like I wouldn't really ever suffer any consequences for my obnoxiousness. I was rarely *high* high but I was almost always impaired to a certain degree.

One night, De Niro invited me to the Monkey Bar, where we'd first met, and he introduced me to Jack Nicholson, who owned the place. A lot of interesting people would hang out at the Monkey Bar: Warren Beatty, Buck Henry, Charles Grodin, different filmmakers. And they were the only people allowed in. No riffraff—unless they were very pretty. Jack would say, "Pretty riffraff is fine with me. Just don't let any cocks in the henhouse—there's already enough in here."

The night I met Jack, a bunch of us, including Sean Penn, went up to his house, and from then on Jack and I became close. For my birthday one year he gave me the Spanish poster for *The Shining* and wrote on it: "To Tom, fellow freedom fighter, more good times."

Being at his house was a trip. He'd say something like "Find someone to give me a cigarette," and four people would jump up to do it. It was like sitting with Picasso for me. I was intimidated but he makes you feel really comfortable.

Marlon Brando lived next door to him, and one time when I was at Jack's, he said, "Hey, kiddo, you wanna meet Marloon? Oh, it's a trip, come on." Jack actually called him "Marloon." Jack nicknames everybody. He called me "Scagmucci" after my character Scagnetti in *Natural Born Killers* because he liked the name Scagmucci better than he liked Scagnetti. He called his assistant "staff." And he called NBA coach Phil Jackson "Cap."

I'll never forget what Brando said to me the night we went to his house: "One day you'll mature and quit acting. Myself, I haven't." That's exactly what he said. I told him, "But I love acting because of you." He took us into a room where he could see all the rooms in his house on video camera, and he'd touch a button and turn a light on, and his dog would chase the lights from room to room. He did that for a long time, and he got a big kick out of it. Then he just got up and walked out—no explanation, no nothing. I think Marlon's father had, for the better part of his young life, excoriated him. Marlon went to New York and became a star so fast, he never really adjusted to it. The sense I got was that he enjoyed the license it gave him to do whatever it was he wanted to do, as I think a lot of us do, but there were parts of the life he had that he never could fully accept.

I met Warren Beatty through Sean Penn; years later, when Warren was looking for an after-hours black nightclub while scouting locations for *Bulworth,* Sean and I went with him. I was pretty much in heaven. And Warren was very funny; he doesn't drink or smoke, and when I asked him why, he just said, very casually, "Because of the way I look." He was very matter-of-fact about it. He told me I should just drink water, and I think I just laughed.

Sean grew up in L.A. but he really wanted to break out of the insular Malibu world that he'd grown up in, so he'd made an effort to know the real Los Angeles—the cultural landmarks. He'd say, "We're going to go to this restaurant in Boyle Heights, to have the best Thai food I've ever had"—that kind of thing. Sean also introduced me to Charles Bukowski. Sean was fascinated with writers and poets and Bukowski actually dedicated one of his books to Sean.

But, as I said, at the same time that all these completely surreal, amazing things were happening in my life, I was also becoming a full-blown heroin addict. And by the time filming wrapped on *Heat,* my problem had only grown worse. When my brother Aaron came out from Detroit to visit me, he saw me doing heroin and coke at night and later found me passed out on the bathroom floor. Even though I never missed a day of work on *Heat* and was never even late, my brother saw that I was in trouble. He told me that he thought I could die any day.

While I was doing all these drugs, I was still juggling a lot of women. But the relationship that was starting to become the most important to me was the one I had with Maeve. And one day I drove over to her apartment on Doheny Drive and basically just said, standing there on her doorstop, "I need you. I'm in trouble and you're the only girl in this town I know who doesn't do drugs and can help keep all these cockroaches away from me."

I had all these sorts of bottom-feeders who were circling me—the type of people who circle everyone who's coming up in Hollywood. People like that can be very pushy, and I could already feel myself acquiescing in ways I didn't want to. Maeve was instrumental in pointing these people out to me and showing me how they were users. And I was just sick of it. I was sick of all the girls, the drugs, the booze—the bullshit. Maeve was the opposite of those people, and I really believed she could protect me from them. And in many ways she did—but that came much later.

That day she said she would help me as a friend but that she couldn't be involved with me romantically. I asked her what I would have to do to get her to actually be with me and she said, "To even get a Chinese dinner, you'd have to go to a thirty-day rehab the day *Heat* wraps," because we'd always go out for Chinese food when we first met. I wanted her back. And I didn't want to be a drug addict. So I said yes to rehab, and her friend got me registered at a place called Sierra Tucson in Arizona for when the movie was over. Sierra Tucson was supposed to be the one rehab you couldn't escape from, but I'd actually heard that Downey had escaped from there—even though it's a thirty-eight-mile walk off of the top of a mountain to get to Tucson after you crawl through a mile of barbed wire. Downey supposedly did it and got on a goddamn airplane in his hospital blues, flew back to L.A., and was in his house in Malibu the same day that Sean Penn and the rest of these guys had put him in Sierra Tucson. I was there for Downey's first intervention, and I knew he was not getting clean. Later, when I'd visit him in prison—I'd go every third Saturday with his old friend Josh Richman—I never in a million years thought I'd end up in prison myself.

Anyway, I agreed to go away. Maeve and I ordered Chinese food, and the stage was set for us to actually be together. Maeve worked with this guy named Glenn, who was my assistant at the time, on making sure I'd actually check into Sierra Tucson. To prove that I was serious I had to send Sierra Tucson a deposit, but I kept making excuses for why I wasn't doing it. So my mom and Aaron flew out once the movie wrapped to make sure I went; the doors were closing in on me. Because I felt trapped, I stopped heroin cold turkey, which of course made me completely dope-sick. I still hadn't sent Sierra Tucson the deposit. That's when Glenn came up with the idea of doing an actual intervention and involving De Niro in it. They knew that if Bob was involved, I wouldn't be able to say no.

So, on June 1, 1995, Maeve dropped me, my mom, and Aaron off at my therapist's office and then called her friend who got me into Sierra Tucson and promised I'd check in there that night. At the same time, Glenn arranged for De Niro to show up at my therapist's. All I knew was that I was sitting in therapy with my mom and brother talking about my drug problem, and suddenly Bob knocked on the door. He came in and said, "Tom, I'm not going to watch you die; I've had friends die." I guess that he was with Robin Williams and John Belushi the night Belushi died, but I have no idea if that's what he was talking about. All I know is that I started weeping. Bob was so empathetic— he really extended himself and projected himself into my drama, which he didn't need to do and which most people wouldn't do. I was just another troubled actor he happened to work with, but he didn't give up on trying to convince me to go to rehab until I said yes.

He said to me that the gig was up and that I was a wonderful actor and he wasn't going to let me die. He asked me, "Don't you want to wake up and know what the hell you're doing? Don't you want to remember what you did last night?" He kept going on and on. Finally he told me, "I love you like you're my son." I didn't want to go to rehab but how could I say no to that?

I went to Sierra Tucson on his private plane and stayed for thirty days. My mom, dad, and brothers Aaron and Paul came to visit, as did Maeve, and I wrote Maeve love letters every single day. I really thought I could stay off drugs and just live a pure, healthy life. When I came back to L.A. clean and sober, Maeve and I really, truly fell in love. It was one of the most romantic summers of my life, and we spent every second together. In many ways, we were the quintessential case of opposites attracting: she was this pristine blonde who'd played at Wimbledon and the French Open. I think I was the third guy she'd ever slept with. Because I was so consumed with her—because we were so consumed with each other—at first it didn't seem all that hard to stay sober. In retrospect, I think I had transferred my drug addiction to a Maeve addiction.

When you're in love, you don't have to do a lot to be perfectly content, and we were no exception. I'd moved from Harratt Street in West Hollywood to Flores Street, just a few blocks away, and she moved in with me the day I got back from rehab. We didn't really leave. I remember she always made fun of me because I was, on the one hand, completely organized, almost to an obsessive-compulsive degree—I liked people to take their shoes off when they came in, and I'd have my freshly pressed shirts in the closet and my glasses lined up just so—but then I'd throw my underwear everywhere. She also used to tell me that I had more beauty products and vitamins than any chick she'd ever known. She was probably right about that.

We spent a lot of time just watching movies, reading books, and listening to music. We also had a trainer whom we shared, and we would exercise together. We actually did everything together; we even shared a cell phone. We got a golden retriever, Seamus, and our whole life was centered on each other and this dog. We'd go on hikes with the dog, walks with the dog, we'd cuddle and play with the dog.

And the two of us had a lot of sex—the most romantic, intense sex of my life. We'd essentially be bawling and telling each other how much we loved each other.

Maeve was like a Rottweiler when it came to making sure I stayed away from drugs. She had my phone number changed. She kept me distracted. And since we were together all the time, there was no way I could have done drugs even if I'd wanted to. We were so attached to each other that we actually preferred a queen-sized bed to a king because that meant there was less room and we'd have to sleep even closer together—there was literally just enough room for us and Seamus. We'd tell each other that when we died, we'd need to be buried together in the same casket. We picked out the names of our future kids and essentially just had the best summer of our lives.

We also developed some rituals back then that we kept for our entire relationship. Our morning routine was to make Irish oatmeal and coffee and then eat it with me sitting on the couch and Maeve in a nearby chair. I'd say, "What's the plan, Stan?" And she'd respond, "I don't know—you tell me, Stanley." And then I'd say, "It's up to the boss; I'm nothing without my Stanley." Usually, after that, we'd go on a hike or to the gym.

Neither of us was much of a cook, but Maeve wanted to learn so one night she made steak. And honestly, it tasted like a doorstop. But it was really sweet how hard she tried and how much she cared about making me a dinner that would make me happy. After that, I asked if she'd cook for us again, and she said, "What are you talking about? The steak I made tasted like a doorstop." And I told her—and I meant it—"Come on, that was the best worst steak I've ever had in my life." Eventually she got better at it and also learned to make some other things, like pasta and this sea bass like the one that they served at Nobu—where we used to go with De Niro a lot back then. She essentially had three dishes, but I learned to love them. I actually came to like them better than anything I could get if we went out to dinner or ordered in, and I was sort of obsessive about her being the one who cooked for me. If my assistant offered to make me a sandwich, I'd say no and ask Maeve to do it.

They say that when you get sober, you have to make that your number-one priority in life, and I wasn't doing that. Maeve was my number one priority and after that came my career. I'd go to the AA meetings in Hollywood, but I only liked to go if she came with me, even though she wasn't an addict and had actually never done drugs in her life. She'd encourage me to go on my own but I felt like I didn't want to be away from her.

Fairly early on in the relationship, I knew I wanted to propose, and, in the fall of 1995, my business manager and I went to a diamond dealer, where I bought a ring. But I decided I would wait to ask her to marry me until sometime during the week between Christmas and New Year's.

She went back to see her family in Chicago for the holidays and was scheduled to come spend New Year's with me in Detroit. But by the time I got to Detroit, the ring was just burning a serious hole in my pocket, and I felt like I couldn't wait a minute longer to ask her.

There was a horrific storm the night she was driving from Chicago to Detroit, and I started to panic that something was going to happen and she wasn't going to make it. So I just sat by the window, waiting and waiting for her to show up. Finally she did. She burst in the door with our dog, saying that she desperately had to pee. I said, "Hold your pee—I have something to ask you!" She went, "No, Tom, I really have to go," and rushed to the bathroom, but I still felt like I couldn't wait to ask her. So while she was in the bathroom peeing, I burst through the door and got down on one knee. I pulled out the ring box and as I was about to ask her, she started saying, "No, no, no." I said, "No? I haven't even finished asking you yet and you're saying no?" And she laughed and said, "No, I meant not when I'm on the toilet! I don't want *this* to be the story we tell our children!" We both started laughing, then she flushed the goddamn toilet, said yes, and we both began crying.

I wanted to get married literally the day after I proposed or at least by May, but Maeve talked me into waiting until the following September. She wanted a long engagement because she wanted to make sure I could stay sober, and she told me that she wouldn't agree to try to have a baby until I'd been sober for at least five years. So we planned this big Irish Catholic wedding in Winnetka, Illinois—where she was from—and I focused on staying clean.

Maeve had started to work a lot more as an actress—she became a regular on the CBS soap opera *The Bold and the Beautiful*—and that meant I had more and more time on my own. And I wasn't great with time on my own. I had a bunch of movie offers being thrown at me at that point, but my agents and managers really wanted me to wait for the right thing. And when I was offered the lead in a horror movie called *The Relic,* we all agreed it was right. I had been offered leads in other movies that I didn't think were any good, and after *Natural Born Killers, Devil in a Blue Dress, Strange Days,* and *Heat,* I decided I wanted to be in something where my character would actually be alive at the end. And I wanted to star in a big Hollywood picture—to prove to people, and to myself, that I could carry one. I was ready to go from being what I called an hour actor to being a two-hour actor.

The Relic was sort of *Alien* meets *Die Hard.* It was about a Chicago police lieutenant who teams up with an evolutionary biologist to track a trail of gruesome murders to the basement of Chicago's Field Museum of natural history, and they realize the killer isn't actually human. I was in New York when I got the offer, and I discussed it with De Niro over lunch. I told him I was worried, and when he asked me why, I said, "Well, I've never had to carry a film." He gave me great advice. He said, "Just take it one scene at a time. Stay healthy, get your rest—and it will happen." So I signed up to do it and got ready by meeting with curators and scientists to learn more about the research that goes on behind public museum exhibits.

I had prepared for *Natural Born Killers* by riding around with the Chicago police. I'd literally put on a bulletproof vest and said, "Take me to the most dangerous places." We went to murder scenes, but I never got shot at; I was actually almost hoping I would, just to see what it felt like. Anyway, because my character in *The Relic* is a Chicago policeman, I used some of what I'd learned back then to inform this role.

The Relic started shooting in Chicago but then continued in L.A., and by the time we got back home, Maeve was on set at *The Bold and the Beautiful* all day. That's when I found myself thinking about heroin again—and not just thinking about it but actually obsessing over it. By then, I'd hired one of Maeve's friends, Carol, to be my assistant. CAA had sent down every hot little twenty-three-year-old they could find when I'd originally decided to hire someone new, but Maeve knew me well. She took one look at what was going on and said, "Oh, no—I've got someone who will work out far better." She introduced me to her friend Carol, whom she'd worked with at a clothing store and who was, most relevantly, a lesbian.

The rule Maeve and I had established was that I wouldn't leave the set of *The Relic* unless Carol was with me. So one day I got smart. I asked one of the extras if I could borrow his car, and then I took it downtown at lunchtime to score heroin. When Maeve came home that night my eyes were pinned, and I had the AC on full blast and was itching everywhere and trying, with every bit of acting skill I could muster, to convince her that I wasn't high.

Of course, it didn't work. She could always tell when I was high; she could literally tell if I'd used by the way I walked up the stairs. So she called Peter Hyams, the director of *The Relic*, and told him that she thought they should do another intervention. She really believed in me and was doing everything in her power to save me. And if anyone could have, it was she; that woman is a force of nature.

So Maeve, Carol, Peter Hyams, and this guy Dallas Taylor—who had once been in Crosby, Stills, Nash & Young but had become an interventionist—did another intervention on me, and I agreed to check into Exodus, a rehab in Marina del Rey, as soon as the shoot wrapped.

I did, as promised, check into Exodus when I was supposed to but I was so defiant that I just picked up and took off after a week—not to go out and use drugs, if you can believe it, but so that I could be home in the bed I shared with Maeve and eat pizza. I'm not kidding. Maeve came home to find me in bed with a Domino's pizza. She drove me straight back to Exodus, and even though I tested clean, they made me start their program over again.

Once I was there, Maeve had all my agents and managers come to visit me and tell me that they couldn't handle my addiction any longer and that if I couldn't stay sober, they were all going to leave my life. I know now that these were all people who loved and cared about me and were terrified by what I was doing to myself—and, by extension, to them. But I was so deluded that I just got angry.

When I finished the program after a month, I relapsed almost immediately. I essentially spent the entire next year at Exodus. I went three times over a period of twelve months. I could stay clean when I was there but as soon as I'd get out, I'd use again. I liked being there, actually, especially because a lot of guys I knew were in there with me—guys like Scott Weiland and Mike Starr. The crazy thing about being in rehab with Mike Starr, God rest his soul, is that he was so high for so long that when we were on *Celebrity Rehab* together fifteen years later, he had forgotten we already knew each other and were friends. If you watch the part of the show where we're introduced and Mike clearly doesn't realize he already knows me, I have the funniest look on my face.

I don't know if it was because Exodus was so hard-core or if everything I'd heard in rehab finally just gelled together in my brain—or if I was just sick of the cycle of cleaning up, only to relapse—but I was eventually able to get sober and then stay clean for the nine months leading up to our wedding. Originally, De Niro was supposed to be my best man but a month before the wedding, he found out that his film was going to open the Venice Film Festival, and he couldn't make it. We actually thought about moving the wedding because of that, but Bob wouldn't hear of it so we just went forward.

Even though I had very solid sobriety at that point, I started to panic about everything going on in my life, and I actually planned to relapse once I got to Chicago—which was where I was flying into for the wedding. So before I went to the airport to go to Illinois, I got up really early in the morning and bought a bunch of heroin. I hadn't done any heroin in a long time, and I bought about two hundred dollars' worth and then threw out about two-thirds of it. I had ten balloons and ended up taking only three or four. I flew to Chicago with my friend Scott, and I was just a bundle of nerves—partially because I was flying with heroin, partially because I knew I was about to do heroin for the first time in a long time, partially because I hate flying, and partially because I was getting married. I was just a mess and ordered a drink the minute I stepped on the plane; I think I'd downed it by the time I sat down.

When we got to Chicago, I made up this bizarre excuse for Scott about having to go to McDonald's and have a burger or something;

in reality I needed to get tinfoil to do the heroin. So we went to the closest McDonald's to the airport, and as I ordered a burger, I said in a whisper to the counter person, "By the way, do you have any tinfoil?" Scott heard me. He knew me really well and understood that my asking about tinfoil meant I was trying to get it to get high. He just said, "Tinfoil? That's it, mister," and led me out of there. I played innocent and tried to convince him that he'd heard wrong or misunderstood what was happening, but he wasn't having it. He just said, "That's it— let's go." He asked me to hand over the dope, and I didn't deny having any, but I didn't hand anything over, either.

The next night, there was a barbecue at Maeve's house, where her family was going to meet mine for the first time. I was, honestly, terrified. Her family is so lovely and respectable and I didn't know how they were going to react to mine. And Maeve knew that the best way to handle the situation would be to tell the bartenders not to serve me any alcohol. But what she didn't count on was that my high school friends from Detroit would all be there, slipping me drinks. Everything went okay between our two families, but I got pretty drunk, which means that I didn't feel like ending the night after the party. So a group of us went out to clubs in Chicago afterward. And I know this sounds bad, but my Detroit friends and I always called each other "nigga"—it was just something we did. So we walked into this nightclub and, completely drunk, I basically screamed, "Where the fuck are all these niggas coming from?" It was one of those movie-like moments where there was complete silence in the place. And then I heard a deep voice from behind me ask, "Now what did you say?" and I saw a big black hand in front of my face. It turned out that, completely randomly, Laurence Fishburne happened to be in town and he was at that club. As he stared down at me, he suddenly realized he knew me. He got this weird look on his face and just went, "Tom? Is that you?" I was, of course, horrified and did my best to try to explain myself, but I was so embarrassed that I ended up getting even more obliterated. By the time I got back to my hotel room that night, I was a complete wreck.

The next morning, Maeve and my mom came to my room and basically said I had to stop drinking or the wedding was off. I promised them that I would stop, and I was determined to keep my word.

That night was the rehearsal dinner, and I had to give this big speech about how Maeve and I met. I was incredibly nervous and think it might actually have gone better if I'd had a drink. But I was stone-cold sober and just sweating up a storm—which is what I do when I'm anxious—and the speech was a disaster. I tried to just talk about how Maeve and I met, but then I delved into this whole thing about how we were dating other people but really had the hots for each other. I was just sweating and sweating, and it was getting worse and worse. Finally, Scott put a hand on my shoulder and said, "I think that's enough."

But then, of course, we got married the next day. It was, I have to say, a really beautiful wedding. My friend Scott filled in for De Niro. Michael Mann was there, as was Michael Wincott, an actor I'd become friends with on *Strange Days*. Ashley Hamilton—whom I'd met through getting sober—and John McGinley and some of our other actor friends also came out for it. Ashley Hamilton actually proposed to Angie Everhart at our wedding, and they got married a few months later. Anyway, after the wedding, Maeve and I flew back to L.A. to bring our dog home and then we went on our honeymoon to Hawaii.

Fairly soon after we were married, we bought a beautiful, 2,800-square-foot, three-bedroom ranch-style house in Benedict Canyon. We looked around some—Maeve looked even as far as Malibu Colony—but we settled on that house, and we completely loved it. It had a pool and a gym, but that wasn't why I loved it. It was just that it was all ours. The house became almost like a living, breathing thing to me. And we chose what to fill it with very thoughtfully. We liked the bed at the Four Seasons, so I actually called the hotel and asked them what kind of beds they had there. Maeve ordered that exact bed, and we attached it to our headboard, which was a hundred-year-old Irish church door. Everything in the house was like that; carefully selected and exactly the way we wanted it.

One of the first investments we made as a couple was in Ago, the restaurant that De Niro, Harvey Weinstein, and a few other people had opened. We were part of a group of investors that included Christopher Walken, Tony Scott, and Ridley Scott. It was truly a spectacular time. *The Relic* ended up doing well—it knocked *Evita* out from the top box-office spot when it came out—and I won the Best Actor award at the Madrid Film Festival.

We had a wonderful group of friends. We would have dinner at Ago with De Niro and his wife, Grace, spend Thanksgiving with Michael Mann, and plan vacations with Mike Medavoy and Sean Penn. Maeve and I also liked to travel together. We went to Hawaii, London, Paris, Dublin, and Venice. And if neither of us was on set, we had breakfast, lunch, and dinner together every day. The problem was when we were apart. I was so in love with Maeve that being around her actually made me forget about drugs. But when I wasn't around her—when she was working more and more on *The Bold and the Beautiful*—that's when things would get dangerous, and I'd relapse.

But whether I was staying sober or relapsing, work continued to go well. I signed with a new manager, Beth Holden, who arranged for me to have a meeting with the director Terrence Malick, who was then putting together *The Thin Red Line,* a World War II movie with Sean Penn. He told me that he wanted to cast me but couldn't decide which part. At the same time, Matthew McConaughey—who was another of Beth's clients—was shooting *Amistad* with Steven Spielberg, so Beth got ahold of the script for the other World War II movie that was floating around town then, *Saving Private Ryan*. She asked Denise Chamian, who was casting the movie, what she thought of me for the part of Sergeant Mike Hovarth. Denise liked the idea but said that Steven was concerned about my relationship with drugs.

Then one day, I got the call: Steven Spielberg wanted to meet with me. But he wanted Maeve to come to the meeting, too. So the two of us went in and sat down with him and the first thing he did was turn to Maeve and ask, "Can Tom stay clean and sober?"

She swore that I could. I swore that I could. My guess is that working with John Belushi on *1941* had made Spielberg cautious about ever working with another addict—though he didn't say that. Steven's a very understanding and loving man. He believes in family and right and wrong and home and hearth and all that good stuff. And because of Steven's experiences in life and the way he was raised in Phoenix and his beginnings in Hollywood, he hasn't forgotten who he is. He never abused drugs even though he was around a lot of them, but he didn't judge people who did. He had a sense of humor, too. I remember him saying at that meeting, "Well, it is a war movie so if you relapse, I guess we could just kill you off at any time."

He also told me he'd loved my performances in *Natural Born Killers* and *Heat* but that he'd always seen a heroic quality in me that had never been explored by a filmmaker, and he wanted to bring that out. He said, "It's like you've been given part of a piano and have only been allowed to play certain notes. I want to give you the whole piano."

The one wrinkle in all of this was that Terrence Malick took my not doing *The Thin Red Line* as a complete betrayal. But he'd never decided which part he wanted me to play, and ultimately, I think I made the better choice.

I had to lose a little weight before I went over to England for *Saving Private Ryan* and we got it put in my contract that production would pay for a trainer for me to lose the weight I needed to in L.A. Because Maeve's story line on *The Bold and the Beautiful* had heated up and she had to be at work there almost every day, she and I tried to figure out what would be the best plan for keeping me clean. After promising Steven that I could stay sober for the shoot, she felt like the best way to get me out of our house—where I had memories of a lot of drug slips—would be for us to go to San Ysidro Ranch for a month. It was our favorite place to vacation, and she knew that if we went there, I could work out with a trainer, eat well, and just be in a peaceful place. So that's exactly what we did. I stayed there, reading, looking at my script, exercising, and hanging out with our dog, while she commuted to CBS in Hollywood every day for work. I actually didn't think about doing drugs and we had a lovely, romantic month there. When we drove back to L.A., I was really proud of myself that I was about to do the best movie of my life clean and sober.

Maeve was working pretty much every day, but her producers agreed to give her two weeks off and then lighten up her story line so that she could easily travel back and forth to England that summer to see me while I was shooting. The problem was that those two weeks didn't start until two days after I was scheduled to leave.

I've always had a serious fear of flying and was borderline convinced that the plane would crash or something bad would happen if Maeve didn't fly with me. I was so irrational that I begged her to fly out with me on a Tuesday, then fly back to L.A. the next day for work, and then fly back again. And I said all sorts of cruel things about how I was making more money than her so she should just blow off her work. I felt sort of irrationally hurt by the fact that she wouldn't come, and I just started striking out in whatever way I could—but she stood her ground and said that she couldn't do it, though she would come to see me when her vacation started. Honestly, I was a spoiled brat back then, and so I left feeling like she'd betrayed me.

When I got to London, I felt bad about how much torture I'd put Maeve through over flying out with me so I called her and said, "I miss you—call me no matter what time it is." Then, as I was going to dinner, I ran into an actress I knew named Charlotte Lewis in the lobby of the hotel. She was in *Coming to America* and was considered sort of the Kim Basinger of her time. And while we're all responsible for our own actions and I'm in no way saying I *wasn't* at fault here, Charlotte was clearly out to seduce me. And, well, she succeeded and the two of us ended up back in my hotel room. As soon as we had sex, I felt terrible and was actually crying quietly into my pillow afterward. Charlotte reached over to cuddle, and I had to move away. And then—well, Maeve called. I felt so guilty and confused and fucked-up that I picked up the phone instead of letting it ring and answered in a sort of whisper. Maeve said, "Oh, you sound like you were asleep—go back to bed and call me tomorrow." And then Charlotte said, in the loudest voice you can possibly imagine, "Who's that?" Maeve of course heard her and asked, "Who's that? Is that the TV?" And I couldn't lie. I just immediately started crying.

Maeve was furious. She paused and then said, "You just made your bed—now you'll have to lie in it." She was absolutely right. I loved this woman with everything in me, and yet I ended up in bed with someone I didn't even like. Maeve was supposed to fly out to London the next day to be with me for part of the shoot, but instead she went to see the divorce lawyer Dennis Wasser. And I guess when she was meeting with him, she was crying so hard that he said to her,

"You're still in love with him, aren't you?" And he suggested that she really think about whether she should move forward with a divorce.

I begged her not to leave me. I got everyone I could to do the same. De Niro called her and told her that she should stick with me, that sobriety was hard and I was struggling and had fucked up but that I loved her. I had to leave for the boot camp we had to do before the movie started, and I was completely devastated. Here I was supposed to be this tough guy and I was crying to all the other guys that she was leaving me. I knew she still loved me, though.

Boot camp was, honestly, fucking awful. I had worked with the guy who ran it—a veteran marine named Dale Dye—on *Born on the Fourth of July* and *Natural Born Killers,* and he was tough.

We had to spend six days in a forest in England, sleeping outside and going through a grueling training regimen. All we had were these World War II–type blankets and rations and Dye wouldn't even call us by our real names—only by our character names. We had to get up at dawn and run five miles every morning in full military gear. It was cold and miserable and I threw up all down my shirt on the first day. But Dye said that we wouldn't be able to portray military discipline if we didn't live it. I knew he had a point but it was terrible. I only ate beans in tomato sauce the whole time. The whole goal of the training was to reprogram us: they were literally trying to take out parts of our personalities and bring out our aggressive nature so we could think like the "killing machines" we were playing.

Maybe it's not all that surprising, but I had a couple of run-ins with Captain Dye. He called Tom Hanks "Turd Number One" and called me "Turd Number Two"—everyone else he just called turds. At one point I said to him, "Don't call me a turd anymore. I don't like it. I'm doing my job out here, and don't do that anymore." He made me do something like two hundred push-ups for that.

Apparently, my manager Beth got a call from one of the producers who said that if I didn't get with the program, they would consider sending out offers to other actors to replace me. I guess the names Bill Paxton and Gary Sinise were mentioned. Beth called me and said, "Look, this is it; if you get fired by Spielberg, you're never going to get another job again." I got right in line after that.

Still, the truth is that we had all been run ragged from boot camp and wanted to quit. At one point, Tom Hanks called a meeting for all of us where he said we should all stick with it. And it turned out that it was really important that we did that because we ended up doing a couple of maneuvers that were difficult and that we wouldn't have learned to do if we'd left. But it rained every fucking day of that boot camp and it was as if Captain Dye had booked the rain especially for us. He'd say, "If it ain't raining, you ain't training. If it ain't snowing, we ain't going!" And "Up the hill, down the hill, fuck the hill, Rangers, Rangers, can't quit, can't quit, don't quit, don't quit, won't quit, won't quit, Rangers, Rangers." We'd run miles singing that shit, which certainly bonded us together.

By the time boot camp was over and we'd all gone to Ireland to begin filming, Maeve had reconsidered the divorce and even agreed to come out to be with me. When she got there, I did everything I could to show her that I could be a better man. I made love to her with the desperation of someone who's dying—because, in a lot of ways, I felt like I would die without her.

I stayed sober throughout the whole production, in large part because Maeve was there with me so much of the time. But I was also white-knuckling it—meaning that I was still thinking obsessively about using heroin and just not allowing myself to do any. It helped that it wasn't exactly easy to get there. I did go out to try to find it once but I had a hard time locating any so I just said, "Fuck it." And I remember one day I was sitting on set just preoccupied with using and someone on the crew who'd had a heroin problem came and sat down next to me and said, "Stop thinking about it." Addicts have this way of being able to read other addicts, and it was like he could tell exactly what I was thinking. I'd talk to that guy at night when my cravings were bad, and that really helped. I also became very good friends with actor Jeremy Davies, and that friendship helped a lot as well.

One day when we were shooting, I twisted my ankle and, about an hour later, it really hurt. And, look, I know myself; I understood that painkillers were a distinct possibility if I went to the doctor. My ankle did really hurt, and it's not like I purposely twisted it in order to go to the ER, but I just think my brain understood that drugs were accessible and that maybe made me think I was in more pain than I actually was. Beth and her sister—who were visiting at the time—took me to the hospital, in Dublin I think, and when the doctor came in, he asked if I was okay or if I needed morphine. I said, "Actually, yes," at the same time as Beth said, "No, he definitely doesn't."

Beth could always make me laugh. One day when she was still there visiting, production moved my trailer from where it had been the entire shoot. I needed to change for a scene, and I started to get upset because I didn't know where I was supposed to go or where my other wardrobe was. Someone handed me an incredibly small T-shirt, but because I was angry, I didn't even really notice its size. I just took off what I was wearing and put that on instead. I was still sort of ranting while wearing this shirt, but then I looked over at Beth and saw that she and her sister were trying to keep from cracking up. That's when I started laughing, and pretty soon we were all howling.

I just kind of fudged my way through staying sober on that shoot. I wasn't going to meetings—I wasn't doing everything right—but I didn't use. And thank God for that because they tested me a lot and there was no cheating these tests—you couldn't get fake urine because you had to go in with no clothes on and no bottles.

My dad hadn't been to many of my movie sets, but he flew to Wexford Island, where he ended up sitting with Tom Hanks for a while, and then he sat with Steven for four days and watched him. I think Steven was kind of fascinated with my father because he saw me one way and then he met my dad, who was this very sophisticated, Harvard-educated, elegantly dressed gentleman.

I had a wonderful time working with Tom Hanks—we were sort of "good Tom" and "bad Tom," and you can guess who was which. We played good friends. In scenes where it was just the two of us, our characters called one another by their first names, and only Rangers who knew each other very well did that. And my character's real purpose in the movie was to keep Hanks's character alive and make sure that the other men didn't see that he was falling apart. At the end of the shoot, Tom wrote me a beautiful note about how he'd never forget making the movie with me.

Saving Private Ryan meant a lot to me. It gave me an opportunity to pay homage and honor and give my respects to the fighting man, to my own family, and to America itself. I don't think we, as Americans, think enough about the men who fight to keep this country free, and I was glad to be a part of something that might inspire people to think about that more. The average age of those men on D-day was eighteen, and it was amazing to me that these teenagers were willing to risk, and sadly often lose, their lives for us. And working with Steven was amazing. Watching him make the D-day scene come to life was unforgettable. He had no storyboards and no shot list; he'd just come out and point to what he wanted. The technicians told us we had two seconds to get past each land mine, and if we were too close to it, we could lose a foot. That helped me sort out my motivation for the scene. The whole experience was extremely rewarding but it was also a very tough shoot. I worked every one of the sixty-one days, although that was actually less than it was supposed to be. We were scheduled to go sixty-eight but finished seven days early.

In between making *Saving Private Ryan* and the release, I packed on forty pounds to play John Gotti in the NBC miniseries *Witness to the Mob*. It was for De Niro's production company, and he said, "Listen, we can do this two ways: you can wear a fat man suit or you can gain the weight." I wanted my character to feel real, and the fact was that Gotti couldn't lay off the cannoli, so I gained the weight. His belly was a sign of his success. He was a big man in every way, and that was his tragic flaw. So I basically went from being in the best shape of my life after *Saving Private Ryan*—I was 180 pounds of all muscle—to being a complete glutton. I ate cream sauce with everything I could get my hands on. I ate lots of pizza, ice cream, meatball sandwiches, and macadamia brittle. I got so fat that at one point, when I was in the shower, I looked down and I couldn't even see my dick anymore. I became such a pig that Maeve said I even started snoring.

I took the weight off—carefully, under a doctor's supervision—to make a smaller, blue-collar movie called *The Florentine,* which was written by my friend Tom Benson and starred people who were all friends of mine: Jeremy Davies, Michael Madsen, Chris Penn, and Maeve. I played a guy who comes back to town and finds out his ex-girlfriend is getting married. I also made a movie called *The Match,* where I played a former air force fighter pilot guy who's become the local drunk in a small Scottish town where he was based during Desert Storm. That was a definite departure from the kind of thing I normally did—it was a sweet little romantic comedy starring Richard E. Grant—but I really enjoyed it.

Then I signed on to a Martin Scorsese movie, *Bringing Out the*

Dead, which starred Nicolas Cage as a burned-out ambulance driver who believes he's seeing the ghosts of people he couldn't save. I played his ex-partner, a real psychopath who's sort of the last thing Cage's character needs at that point. I relocated to New York to do it. It was a lot of night shoots and I didn't get along at all with Marc Anthony—the guy who would go on to marry Jennifer Lopez but back then played this crazy homeless guy in the film. During one scene, he was lying on a stretcher in the ambulance when I was fighting with him and very suddenly and unexpectedly the IV and all the stuff that was hanging above him fell and hit him in the balls. He blamed me for that and started swearing and yelling at me. Production had to literally pull us apart.

When I returned to L.A., I once again struggled to stay sober. One night Maeve and I went out to dinner with producer Brad Bell and his wife at Asia de Cuba, which had opened out of the pool bar at the Mondrian Hotel. I kept slipping away, saying I was going to the bathroom, but I was actually just going to the bar and ordering drinks. Because I was drunk, when I ran into a friend of mine named Michael Stone, I invited him to come over afterward. Maeve knew that Michael and I would do drugs together, and she put her foot down. She said, "If he comes over, I swear to God I'm calling nine-one-one."

When we got home, Michael rang the bell so Maeve—true to her word—started to dial 911. She was sitting on the couch with the phone, and I tried to kick it out of her hand but accidentally kicked her in the neck instead. I started apologizing as she hung up the phone and then Michael walked in the door. The phone started ringing, but we ignored it while Maeve told Michael and his friends that they had to leave because she didn't want drugs in the house. Michael said he understood and that he hadn't known that I was trying to stay clean. But the phone call we hadn't picked up was 911 calling back, which is what they do if you call them and hang up. And if you don't pick up, apparently they show up at your house. Suddenly six cops were at my door.

Even though I'd been drunk, I was suddenly sober as could be. It's like how if you're drunk and get in a car accident, you suddenly feel completely sober. I was arrested and taken to the West Hollywood sheriff's department. Still, I bailed out right away, and life kept moving forward.

I'd have periods of sobriety, but chemicals just had such a hold over me. It was always the same old story: I'd get sober, have a few good weeks and go to meetings and show everybody that I was sober. And then I'd have something like a glass of wine. That would turn into three bottles of wine, which would turn into heroin. I've always had a very strong constitution. My friend Scott used to say that he would see me put away more liquor than he'd ever seen anyone drink, and then I'd bounce out of bed the next morning, ready to face the day. Of course, whenever I'd relapse, at first I'd always try to convince everyone I was still sober—I think some of the best acting I've ever done in my life, in fact, was pretending I was sober when I was high as a kite. But after a while, everyone would always catch on.

Maeve hated all the dope street lingo and thought that it was all part of the addiction, so she'd never call anything by those words— she called balloons "tomatoes," for example. Our whole marriage was fraught with problems because of my relationship with heroin. I kept thinking I could stay sober without going to meetings, but she thought I needed to go, so to ensure that I went, she'd go with me. But then she began to learn about codependency and realized that it wasn't healthy for her to be doing that because it just made me rely on her to stay sober. She started going to Al-Anon and left me to go to AA meetings on my own, but I just couldn't seem to commit to them.

Like I said, Maeve could always tell when I'd slip up. At one point, she found out I was taking Vicodin, which I'd gotten from a Doctor Feelgood guy I'd met at the gym. She tore that guy a new asshole, but I continued to get away with taking it. I think, subconsciously, I would sometimes be purposely sloppy in trying to cover my tracks so that she'd catch me and I'd thus have to stop the cycle—at least temporarily.

Finally, one day she said she thought I should go on methadone so that I could be weaned off opiates and wouldn't then try to get ahold of Vicodin when I wasn't doing heroin. I thought it would be like a regular methadone clinic—where you have to wait in line forever and people would see me there, so I told her, "I can't go to the methadone clinic, Maeve. Heroin addiction isn't chic." She said, "You just don't want to stand in line, you dick. You say the reason you can't go is that you're famous, but that's not what you're thinking about; you're really thinking about the inconvenience of standing in line." When she said things like that, I'd think, "This woman knows me better than I know myself." Because it was true. I really just didn't want to have to wait an hour in line. But she said, "I've handled it." She'd called Dallas Taylor, the guy who'd led the intervention that put me in Exodus the first time, and he'd told her about a hospital in Century Park where they'd give you whatever amount of methadone you needed. The woman who ran the place was named Caroline Perry. People said she over-charged, but she had enormous success.

The first day I went there, I lied to Caroline. I somehow got her and Maeve to do what they had to do, but then when I got Caroline alone, I said, "I lied to you, Miss Perry, because my wife was here. I'm using a lot more than I said I was in front of her." They were going to give me 80 milligrams of methadone and I told her, "Giving me eighty milligrams is like giving me, if I was a cow, one piece of straw or blade of grass. I need a field." So she upped it to 200 milligrams, which is the highest amount you can ever get. The way they give you methadone is they put it in Tang juice, because you can't get high off of it when it's diluted that much, and the sugar in the Tang makes it difficult to cook the juice down if you wanted to inject the methadone.

I would advise anyone not to get on methadone, because it's really difficult to get off of. It's supposed to be curing you of heroin addiction, but you just become addicted to methadone. If you're on a high dose, you can't get out of bed unless you have it. You feel high on it but the high isn't nearly as good as a heroin high. You feel some contentment and some sedation but you don't get any of the euphoria you get from heroin—which is, of course, the best part of heroin. At first you feel stimulated, but as time goes on, you just feel sort of lethargic. I'd say being on methadone means feeling better than normal but not quite high.

I stayed on methadone that way for two years, eventually walking down the ladder from 200 milligrams to 100 to none, but Miss Perry knew a lot of it was psychosomatic for me, so they didn't even tell me when I was off. They just kept giving me Tang without any methadone in it. I actually drank the Tang for some seventy-one days and when I got home from shooting *Big Trouble,* they finally told me I was off methadone. And even when I knew the truth, I still wanted my Tang. It was bizarre. The whole thing was so mental.

Then, on Easter of 1998, Maeve and I flew back to Detroit, since my younger brother Paul, who'd started acting by then, was starring in a play there. Maeve flew from Detroit to see her family in Chicago because she had to take her mom to get a CAT scan. And what they found out from the CAT scan was that her mom, Mary—a completely amazing woman I loved like she was my own mom—had stage-three ovarian cancer. Maeve and I were both stunned by the news, and soon after, she went back to Chicago to be with her parents for three weeks while her mom went through chemotherapy. My brother Aaron came out to stay with me—essentially, to keep an eye on me—while Maeve was in Chicago, but I had a short window of time between when Aaron was there and when Maeve was coming home, and I essentially planned a combined methadone and heroin relapse. When I got it in my head that I wanted to get high, I'd start scheming a way to make it happen: I'd figure out when I was going to be alone and how I could get ahold of as much heroin or methadone—or whatever it was—as possible. It didn't really matter how much time I'd had sober or how much better my life had gotten since I'd been clean: when the idea got in my head, there didn't seem to be anything I could do to stop it, and all rational thought—about what I'd be losing if I relapsed or about how much I'd disappoint people—flitted away. In a way, planning a relapse was almost a high in itself, since it took me out of the moment I was in and into a state of euphoric anticipation. And the night that Maeve returned from Chicago, her friend picked her up at the airport and then took her to a surprise girls' dinner that she'd planned to help cheer her up about what was going on with her mom, so that left me even more time.

Carolyn Perry had given Aaron four or five days' supply of methadone and I had watched him like a hawk to see where he was going to hide it. Even though I hadn't seen exactly what he did with it, eventually I found it. So I took the methadone, more than I should have, the morning Maeve was coming back. I took some more during the day. And when Aaron was gone, I took the heroin. Within a second, I knew I might be in trouble; it was very strong and I was gone.

Maeve had a feeling something was wrong when she called from the restaurant and I didn't answer the phone. She drove home immediately, and as she was coming up the canyon, she grew a bit more frantic. When she came into the house and turned on the light in the bedroom, she saw me lying there snoring, but it was a slow, weird snore that she'd never heard before. She tried to wake me up, but I wouldn't wake up, so then she started shaking me and pushed me over. I was out. She called 911—I heard the tape later—and very calmly said, "I'm at 2761 Hutton Drive, my husband has overdosed, and I'm almost certain it's on heroin." The person on the other end said, "Ma'am, what does he look like? Turn him over, pound on his back, clear up his lungs, and now check for a pulse. We'll be there any minute; they're driving up the mountain now." She said my pulse was really slow, and I looked gray. Maeve had never been around drugs and yet she somehow had the presence of mind to turn me over on my stomach and clear my throat.

The ambulance got there and they threw me on a gurney. All I know is that I came to at Sherman Oaks Hospital, where the doctor took me by the chin and said, "You were dangerously close to suffering from brain damage, and you owe your wife your life so stop fucking bullshitting with us, stop fucking around, and let us fix you." It was a terrible, terrible overdose. I was in the hospital for a while afterward. When I'd call the nurse, by the time she walked in the room I'd have forgotten what I'd wanted to ask her. They told me it was going to take some time for my short-term memory to return, and even when I got home from the hospital I was still having a lot of trouble remembering things. But I got clean right away after that. I took a little bit of methadone for a couple of weeks, and then I was done.

They were right about my short-term memory. When I was first back home from the hospital, I'd go to the pool to go swimming and forget what I went outside for, then come back into the house. Maeve would find me crying in the front room. She'd ask, "What's wrong?" And I'd say, "I can't remember. Why did I do this to myself? What did I do to myself?" I had scared myself straight. I did not want to die. I was glad to be alive, but it took a good three months for my mind to return and for me to be able to even concentrate enough to read a few pages of a book.

But I was determined this time. Maeve's mom was still sick then, and one day Maeve said to me, "Look, my mom has a fifty-fifty shot of making it at this point, and the fact is, if she could go to a meeting that would help her cure her cancer, she'd go to twelve a day." That really impacted me because I truly loved Maeve's mom. I started going to meetings and became completely consumed with staying sober. I think I almost started to believe that if I stayed clean, Maeve's mom would be okay. And her cancer did end up going into remission, which was a genuine fucking miracle—I mean, they really didn't think she was going to make it and she pulled through; in fact, she's still alive today. I was very close to her, and I'd have conversations with her where she'd say, "Please pull yourself together, Tom—please pull yourself together for my daughter." I don't think there's any single thing that ever motivated me to stay sober more than that.

In the midst of all this, in the summer of 2000, I left to do *Pearl Harbor*. I had originally met Ben Affleck back in the late 1990s at a tattoo shop, when I went up to him and told him that the speech he'd given at the Oscars for *Good Will Hunting* was the best speech I'd ever heard by a young person, and it was really reminiscent of a young politician. I don't know how many people remember that speech but basically Matt Damon got up there and started giggling, and Ben just took the mic and started thanking Harvey Weinstein and Robin Williams in this very confident and smooth way. I actually told him that he reminded me of John F. Kennedy Jr. We became friends from there and he taught me to play poker—although, I have to admit, not very well.

Ben was going through some personal trouble in the making of *Pearl Harbor* and the producer, Jerry Bruckheimer, asked me to go talk to him. There was an enormous amount of pressure on Ben for that movie. Josh Hartnett couldn't carry it—it was one of his first leading roles. Kate Beckinsale couldn't carry it. The job was resting squarely on Ben's shoulders, and I think director Michael Bay made that fairly clear. Ben looked like he was in danger of cracking under the pressure, and I went and said to him, "Look, man, you can't fuck up and throw everything you have away. You have a chance to have the brass ring and if you fuck up, you'll regret it." I don't know how much of an impact my speech had on him but he did end up getting his shit together.

Right after that, I left to do *Red Planet*—a futuristic movie with Val Kilmer about a team of American astronauts on the first manned trip to Mars—in Jordan and Australia. It was a brutal shoot. It was hot as hell and the script was sort of being rewritten as we went. Now, Val always had a reputation for being hard to work with—he supposedly burned a camera operator's face on *The Island of Dr. Moreau*—but we'd gotten along well on *Heat*. But this time, it was a whole different story.

Basically, the movie came along quickly and I needed to lose a little bit of weight because I was still carrying around what I'd gained for *Witness to the Mob*. So I got it written into my contract that production would pay for my elliptical machine to be sent out to where we were shooting. We started in Jordan and my elliptical was there but Val never saw it. When the movie moved to Australia, he finally saw this elliptical machine in my room and said, "What the fuck is that?"

I was surprised—we'd been friends ever since *Heat*, and he was one of the main reasons I'd signed on to the movie. But he'd been difficult on this movie in general. We were about six weeks into production at this point, and he'd started making it a habit of not coming out of his trailer if he didn't like a particular scene. One day he didn't come out for half a day—not until the scene that was being shot was rewritten until he was written out of it, which wasn't the easiest thing in the world to do. He would keep us waiting an average of three or four hours on days when he'd have the director, Antony Hoffman, in his trailer reworking the script. At one point I said to Antony, "Stop going to his trailer to rework the script." And he said, "I can't—he's the lead in my movie." I responded, "No, he's not—he's the lead in your demolition."

That day, with the elliptical machine, I just said to Val, "What do you mean? You know what it is."

He responded, "I know what it is but what's it doing here?"

His attitude was starting to piss me off, so I just sort of taunted him with "Well, it's an inanimate object so I don't think it talks but why don't I ask it?" Then I walked up to the elliptical and I said, "Hey, what are you doing here?"

He completely snapped. "Fuck you," he said, and he threw a lighter at me. I was in shock. And then he started to say incredibly mean things—he called me names and said, "I'm making ten million on this; you're only making two." It may sound silly but he really hurt my feelings. I've always felt some shame about the fact that I came from a poor family, and someone like Val—who had always been a part of the elite and had been a revered actor since he went to Juilliard—was the kind of person I always felt the most inferior around. He knew that and took this opportunity to rub it all in my face. So for him to bring that up, in that tone and manner, just made me snap. And when I snap, I react with a real fight-or-flight instinct. At that moment, fight was winning, so I picked up the nearest thing to me, which happened to be a fifty-pound weight, and threw it at him. This was, of course, wrong. I regret it and the only thing I can say in my defense is that I wasn't trying to hit him with it; I was just trying to fight back.

He stormed off and I immediately went to his hotel room and knocked on his door, but he wouldn't answer it. I kept banging on the door, but he wouldn't let me in and that's when I really got pissed. I screamed, "Okay, I'm now your enemy and you don't want me as your enemy—trust me!"

In retrospect, the situation was bound to get problematic, and if anyone had thought out some of the arrangements we made ahead of time, they would have known that. For instance, Vera Mitchell was Val's personal makeup artist. She had worked on *Gandhi* and *A Passage to India* and *Heat*, and was widely considered the best in the business. When they were originally working out everything for *Red Planet*, they asked Val if he minded if Vera did my makeup as well. He said he didn't but then, once we were there and it was about 100,000 degrees and everything was tense because he wasn't coming out of his trailer and we were all on edge, he clearly *did* mind. At one point, I asked Vera to come over to touch me up and Val said, "No, Vera, you come here!" And he turned to me and said, "Stop saying her name!"

But when we were shooting, we would both try to be professional and do our scenes. That is, until we moved to our last location, the Fox lot in Sydney. There were sandstorms and it was hot as hell, and by the last week we were there, he was refusing to come out of his trailer at all. Now, Australia had been a penal colony, so our local crew was made up of some tough guys who just didn't know what to do with all this dramatic, crazy-actor bullshit. And it was a first-time director on the movie, who was clearly in over his head. So they asked me, of all people, to go to Val's trailer and ask him to please come out.

He opened the door, but I was drinking a cup of coffee when I walked in and he said, "No drinking in my trailer"—even though he himself was drinking a cup of coffee at the time. So I dumped the coffee and tossed the Styrofoam cup on the ground outside the trailer, planning to pick it up when I left his trailer. He said, "Litterbug. Go pick that up."

That's when I snapped again. I was wearing my space jacket because we'd been in the middle of shooting a scene, but I took it off and said, "Look, Val, we're no longer on Mars. Now we're back on earth. And here on earth, I'm going to beat the shit out of you." His assistant walked up and said, "Hey, Tom, why don't you go?" And then she ran and got my assistant, Carol. Carol coaxed me back to the set.

The next day he kept us waiting nine hours—on a twelve-hour day. When he came out, we shot a scene where he needed a certain prop, and he handed it off to the prop girl rather than holding on to it when he had to do another take. Then he called the prop girl to get the prop again and I guess he felt she wasn't fast enough. This was an eighteen-year-old, completely defenseless girl on her first job, and when she walked up with the prop, Val called her a dumb bitch and then flicked a lit cigarette at her, which actually burned her chest. It was one of the most heinous acts I'd ever seen a person do, and I'd seen a lot of heinous acts in my life.

I'd finally had it. One of the producers who knew how tense the situation was getting had called my manager Beth and said, "Listen, if it comes to blows between Tom and Val, can you ask Tom to not hit Val in the face? Because that might be hard to cover with makeup." Since I knew I couldn't hit him in the face, I hit him as hard as I could in the chest, and he fell down. I remember Simon Baker just going, "Fuuuuuuck." I continued to hit him in the chest, stomach, and arms.

This whole thing was obviously frightening for everyone on the set, but at the same time, I think a lot of people had wanted to punch Val themselves for quite a while. Because of the delays Val was causing, we were going over our allotted time, which meant that a lot of the crew people, who were all planning to work on the *Matrix* sequel, were losing those jobs.

Mark Canton, who was one of the producers on the movie, flew out from L.A. the next day. The day's shoot had been canceled so Val could go to the doctor. He had made it sound to anyone who would listen like I had completely incapacitated him, but he was fine; I doubt he could even get a painkiller prescription. But he took out a restraining order against me, which made finishing the movie challenging; still, we managed.

The truth is, both Val and I were going through terrible times with our wives. I was struggling with my sobriety, which was growing incredibly hard on Maeve. I knew she still loved me, but I also knew that she was getting close to not being able to put up with much more. And when I flew home for a weekend during *Red Planet*, we went to a barbecue and got into the blowup to end all blowups. I went back to Australia assuming we would patch things up the way we always did, but this time I was wrong.

In November 1999, she filed for divorce. I'm not even sure I can describe what that felt like, except to say that if I'd been punched in the gut and had my insides eviscerated, it probably would have felt better.

Val was going through a terrible time with his wife, Joanne Whalley, and they were actually in the process of finalizing their divorce during the shoot. If we'd both been able to just talk about what was going on and tell each other how much we were hurting, I bet a lot of this could have been avoided. But I didn't tell anyone on the set what was going on with Maeve—I kept it all bottled up inside and then allowed it to flare out in these unhealthy ways—and for that, I'm very sorry.

Val and I actually talked about all of this at the *Red Planet* premiere and made up and even became friends again. But back then, by the time I got home from the shoot, a few weeks before Christmas, Maeve had moved into an apartment—taking our dog with her—and wouldn't even tell me where it was. She flew to Dublin to be with her family for Christmas, and I called her every day that she was gone, begging her to reconsider and come back.

When she returned to town, she agreed to see me, but only if I met her at her therapist's office. We went to therapy every single day for three weeks—trying to work everything out. Finally the therapist said that she thought we were ready to go out for a date. I had just been nominated for a Golden Globe—for an HBO movie called *Witness Protection*—and Maeve and I agreed that going to the award show together would be an ideal date.

I didn't win, and then, to add insult to injury, my mom called and told me that when the camera was supposed to show me when they announced my name as a nominee, it actually flashed on someone else. On top of that, I had expected that Maeve would want to come back home after the show, and she didn't. I was beginning to finally accept, for good, the fact that I was really losing her. I asked her if she'd spend the upcoming Valentine's Day with me, and she said no.

The divorce proceedings, which had begun in late 2000 and were halted while we were in therapy together, resumed. I was traumatized.

When it came to the women I truly loved, I always picked people who were better than me—I think to make up for something I felt I lacked. Both Maeve and my girlfriend in graduate school, Michelle, were extraordinarily good women. With both of them, I was initially attracted to how pretty they were, but what I couldn't have consciously known at the time was how tough they both were as well. They were the kind of women who would say no and mean it. When Maeve left, I would think about how much tougher she was than me. I'd think about one night, when a friend of hers was over and we were all drunk, the friend followed me to the bathroom and said she wanted to have a ménage à trois with us. Because I was buzzed and because I'm a guy, I thought it was a great idea, and so the friend and I went up to Maeve—all giggling and everything—and asked her what she thought. She said, "I won't do that," and suddenly the evening went from being funny and playful to being incredibly serious, with that friend being escorted out the door and me being directed to sleep on the couch. I remember feeling that night like I was being scolded like a little kid, but I was also nearly in awe of someone who had enough strength to say, "I won't do that." I had never had any boundaries like that—any lines I'd ever drawn or things I'd decided I wouldn't do—and most everyone I knew didn't, either. That was one of the many things I dwelled on about Maeve as I stayed alone in the house and wept for the six months after she left.

I couldn't have sex with anyone for a very long time, nor could I even conceive of it. I tried to do so, right when she left me—I tried to sleep with an old girlfriend—but when she took off her clothes, I just started crying because it was so jarring. I wasn't on drugs or anything—I was on air, trying to breathe my way through being heartbroken. Luckily, my ex understood; she wrapped a sheet around me as I cried, in heaving sobs. I eventually just accepted that it was going to take time to get over the dissolution of my marriage.

CHAPTER 5

HEIDI

FOR A LONG time, I walked around in a constant state of depression. "Walking around" is actually overstating matters: for nearly a month, I was too depressed to even leave my house. And once I could, I was very much the walking wounded: I wasn't dissolving into tears every second but I was in active pain and looking for any way possible to escape it.

Near the end of January 2001, I found a way. I had met Heidi Fleiss years earlier, in the late 1980s, when she was around the whole Hollywood scene, before she was arrested. Crazy as it may sound, I'd actually always had something of a crush on her. She was really pretty then, as well as funny, smart, and sassy—not remotely what she seems like today. That January night I had been at a barbecue with Jeff Greene, a very successful real estate developer who hung around with a bunch of celebrities. I knew he was friends with Heidi, so I told him that he should call her and have her meet us at Las Palmas, a club that was big at the time. So he called her and invited her out, and when she pulled up outside in her Ford Explorer, I jumped out of Jeff's car and into hers. She was shocked and asked me what the hell I was doing. I just said, "All I want is three weeks of your undivided time." She laughed and said, "I have three hours." Then she looked at me and asked, "What the hell do you want with me anyway? I'm every man's nightmare." I said, "Well, haven't you heard? I'm a nightmare, too."

The flip side of my depression has always been excitement: if I could get excited about something, all the sad feelings that were crippling me would fall away. And, partly because of who she was and partly because of what she represented, Heidi Fleiss seemed exciting to me. That night, we went into Las Palmas and partied with Hugh Hefner and a whole bunch of rock stars. Heidi and I got a table, had drinks, and flirted, and different people were coming and going from our table there all night. I ended up inviting a whole bunch of them over to my house afterward to continue the party, but you never really know with those kinds of things who's going to show. I asked Heidi for a ride home from Las Palmas, and when we got to my place, I invited her inside. As I was giving her a tour, all these people suddenly descended on my house—somewhere around two hundred people, including some of Heidi's former girls. It turned into a crazy night.

Looking back, I believe I thought my depression had lifted but in fact it had just been replaced by something far more dangerous. And if I'd known what crystal meth was going to do to me, I never would have tried it.

Of course, crystal affects people differently, but the way it affected me is by making me want to have sex with every woman on earth. I already wanted to, anyway: I've always had a very strong libido. Later, when my life really fell apart, a guy who was temporarily acting as my manager put out this story that I had a condition he referred to as priapism, where I was never sexually satisfied. That's not true, but I've always been rapacious.

Heidi and I were seeing each other fairly regularly by the time I left for Morocco to shoot *Black Hawk Down* during the summer of 2001. So whenever I had eight or more days off in a row on the shoot—which happened twice—I would come back to L.A. and stay with her. Even though I didn't see it this way at the time, I was also coming back in order to do a lot of meth. Heidi was the one who had it—I didn't know how to buy it or anything. Because she was so much more familiar with the drug than I was, she would do her best to not let me go overboard: she wouldn't let me stay up all night on it and she essentially wanted us both to use it wisely and not the way she'd used it in the past. I was lying to myself, of course, but I thought I was just using a sort of aphrodisiac; I didn't realize I was simply transferring my former heroin addiction to another drug. But my love affair with meth didn't begin in earnest until I was done with *Black Hawk Down;* on set, I mostly stayed sober by playing a lot of chess with Ewan McGregor. He beat me something like 664 games in a row.

Once Heidi and I really started dating, all we did together was watch TV and movies. In many ways, it was just a normal relationship. She'd said to me at the beginning, "I don't care what we do, as long as we don't watch *Martin*," because, she told me, when you're in prison, the black inmates usually run the dayroom, and they want to watch *Martin* all day. When I went to prison later, I learned firsthand that she was right. Male or female, the situation is the same: the blacks want to watch *Martin,* the whites want to watch *Cops,* and the Mexicans want to fight outside.

She lived on Franklin Avenue by Gower Street and we'd walk over to the Mayfair market, buy all these juices, and then come back to her house. It was all very wholesome. One day, we went and bought a fan at Home Depot together. I'm not kidding—that's how boring and basic our day-to-day activities were. It was really hot this one day and her place didn't have air-conditioning, so we went to Home Depot for a goddamn fan. I hadn't done something like that in a long time because I'd become a spoiled movie star with an assistant. I'm not kidding—I didn't go into a grocery store for eight years and when I did, I was so overwhelmed by all the options that I just said, "Fuck it, I'll go home." But that day was so simple and so nice. We went back to her place, turned on the fan, and watched a movie; the whole thing was incredibly romantic.

The fan broke just ten days later, and I think that was the last we ever spent time at her house. She essentially just moved in with me. One day, when we were walking down the street, I looked at her and was struck by this sudden and strong conviction that I loved her. Just as I realized it, I said it out loud—I went, "Fuck, I love you." She looked over at me, very slowly, and said, "I know." Then she paused and said, "I love you, too." Honestly, I was as surprised as anyone: that's why the sentence started with the word *fuck*. I'd never been with a woman who was a convict and prostitute before. And I'd always liked girls that were more classically pretty. But at the same time, loving her almost empowered me. I felt like I'd been trying to fit some mold I didn't really match—in Hollywood, in the world—before then: I'd tried marrying the beautiful blonde, the First Lady type of woman, and it hadn't worked. In retrospect, I just married my First Lady— Maeve—too soon. I should marry her now, though she wouldn't have me now. But being with Heidi felt right back then.

She was already embittered and caustic but she was also a lot of fun. And I think I knew her in a way that no one else did, except maybe her sister. She was meant to have a much different life than she ended up having: if she hadn't gotten sidetracked by money and drugs, I think she would have ended up running a major corporation. She's from an excellent, successful family. She just got off track.

I was with her when she was dealing with her parole and it was the first time I ever knew anyone in that situation. I saw very clearly that the system was set up for people to fail. There's no way anybody can keep all those appointments, particularly parolees who don't have any money and don't have cars; you just can't get to all these places they make you go to get drug tested or to all the meetings they want you to make. When I realized that, I decided that I wasn't going to let her fail. I saw her parole officer fuck with her, too: he'd call her at 9 A.M. and say, "You have to be here in twenty minutes or I'll violate you," when he knew she lived eighteen minutes away. It's not against the law to be late, unless your parole officer tells you, "If you're late, you're going back to prison."

Heidi could be very charming, and she was chastened by what she'd been through. She was walking around with a big *W* for *whore* on her chest, and it brought her down. I didn't think that what the criminal justice system did to her was right. Yes, she did things that were illegal, but I didn't think it was fair that only she got in trouble— not the other girls, nor any of her customers.

There were days when she would say, "I can't do it anymore. I should just go back to prison—it's what they want." It was horrible. I was in love with her, and I saw her try so hard to meet these conditions for her parole, and when she could meet them, they'd just make it harder. But they didn't know she had a secret weapon: me. They'd say, "You have to pay restitution—you owe us eighteen hundred bucks." If she didn't have it, I'd pay it. Anything they wanted, money-wise, I gave to them. There were mornings when we were in Benedict Canyon and had to race down that fucking mountain and we'd get there with four seconds to spare. I did everything I could to get her off parole, which is why in the end her betrayal hurt so much.

When I first told my manager Beth that I was seeing Heidi, her reaction was pretty much this: "Out of all the women in the world, this is the one you pick? Isn't there someone else you could date?" Beth was fairly adamant about the idea that my relationship with Heidi be kept out of the press at all costs, but stories about the two of us started popping up in the *National Enquirer*. People told me they thought Heidi was feeding the *Enquirer* stories about us, but who knows? I wasn't exactly hiding the fact that I was with her.

Beth ended up really coming around on Heidi and seeing what a nice person she could be, but she still maintained that the fewer people who knew about our relationship, the better. She would say, "You're in line to be the next Gene Hackman or De Niro, and the movie business is a sheep business; you really are your image, and you have to stay on the right side of things." Of course, she was right.

But I was having a real honeymoon with both meth and with Heidi. The two were very tied together in my mind and later, it felt like both turned on me at the same time. For roughly the first year and a half that I was with Heidi, it was an honest-to-God good relationship—or at least as good as a relationship between two people on meth could be. The truth is, we weren't actually doing it all that much together. I was always very private with my drug use—that was part of my paranoia. I did drugs alone, whether I was living with people who did the same drugs or not. I think I was always so deeply ashamed of the fact that I was doing drugs at all, that doing them by myself allowed me to be in some sort of denial; people wouldn't talk to me about drugs if they didn't know whether I was doing them and I could just pretend that I wasn't. The truth is, because we weren't really doing the meth together, I don't actually know how much she was using.

In my mind, I was doing well. I felt like I'd gone from being this guy who was very depressed and half dead after his wife left him to someone who was very much alive and very, very virile. On a certain level, I knew that what I was doing was bad—that all drugs are bad for you—and I did everything in my power to avoid thinking about that. I felt like I was coming-to after having the gauze of heartbreak over my face. Drugs work; that's why they're such a big problem. Anyone who says drugs don't work isn't getting ahold of good drugs.

When Heidi moved in with me up at Benedict Canyon, we set up ground rules and one of the main ones was that it was pretty much an open relationship. I knew what she'd done for a living, and I didn't have a lot of sexual jealousy. Maybe I'm a weirdo, but my attitude was I don't give a fuck if you suck off the fucking Lakers as long as you come home to me. It was a decadent time; threesomes were common, and I once had six women in bed with me at one time. I had always been very focused on girls and sex but there was something about meth that transformed general ideas I had about how I wanted to sleep with as many women as possible into a reality. I also think when you're letting yourself fall deep into a hole with drugs, whatever reins you have on other aspects of your life can easily disintegrate.

Heidi and I started to fight about the other women but we fought about other things as well. When I went on Howard Stern to promote *Black Hawk Down,* I arranged for her to come with me so that she could promote her book *Pandering.* And Heidi made a big thing on the air about how she didn't like *Black Hawk Down,* which was just about the worst thing she could have done. I took her as my date to the premiere, which didn't do anything to help make anyone take the movie seriously. Originally, the movie's producers had talked about doing an Academy Award campaign for me but they never did. Instead the film just sort of came and went and didn't end up doing anything for me. I think Beth was right about the sheep mentality and the fact that my association with Heidi meant I was losing credibility.

I stopped doing meth before making a TV movie with Ving

Rhames called *Sins of the Father*—mostly because I was afraid of taking it with me on the plane to Canada and getting busted. Earlier in my career, when I was addicted to heroin, I'd FedEx drugs ahead of time. But I really knew my way around heroin—I knew where to get it, how to handle it, and how to move it around. And I also knew I could get methadone legit from a clinic so I wouldn't get sick. This was a whole different game. Plus, being addicted to meth is nothing like being addicted to heroin. I couldn't do meth and work the way I could on heroin. On meth, you look like hell, you feel like hell, and the only reason you stay up is to do more meth, which makes you look more and more like hell. You also start acting very strange. I was keeping to myself on *Sins of the Father,* and I while I could still act, I didn't look good. My instincts were dulled, and I could feel it.

I came home and started doing meth again but then stopped using before my next movie, *Swindle.* But when I got back to Canada for *Swindle,* I called Heidi and said, "I don't want to feel this low-energy, what can I do?" The truth is that I felt like my ass had fallen three stories down, and I was carrying four hundred pounds on my back. We were really in love at this point, and she was very upset that I was in that state, but she knew meth. She said, "I understand. Now listen to me. I'm sending a girl up there with a large amount of the stuff. But just so you feel better now, you already have some." She explained she'd actually slipped some into a Visine bottle in my toiletries case. She talked me through how to get it out: you squirt it on any surface—glass, preferably—and you just wait and the water evaporates and it turns back into fucking speed. It's amazing. Twenty minutes after you put it there, the atmosphere just sucks up the water and there the meth is in its original form. I was relieved, of course, but it wasn't much—just three or four lines.

The woman she sent up with drugs—a friend of ours—got there

the next day. She'd emptied a bunch of sports pills, then cut up meth so finely that it looked like the white stuff in the middle, put that back in there, then resealed the bottle like it had never been opened. The girl ended up coming back and doing the same thing again during the shoot, and since no one's going to fly to Prince George, British Columbia, and then fly out the next day unless they're doing something that's not right, we acted like she was my girlfriend. She'd check into my room and sleep on the rollaway bed for two nights. When I went to work, she'd kick around the hotel.

To many people, I'm sure this would sound like an odd way to express your love but that's how Heidi showed me she cared about me—by making sure I always had enough meth.

THE LONGER I was with Heidi, the more open our relationship became. What I mean by that is that my house essentially became something of a very well-appointed flophouse for hookers—ones I met, of course, through her. And I was a very understanding landlord.

All these girls were under twenty-five and beautiful. When you're thirty-nine and these gorgeous twenty-three-year-old girls are offering to suck your cock, you don't say, "No way, get out of here, I've got to read the Bible." At least you don't if you're me. I was meeting most of them through Heidi, and they were just around all the time.

I'd also met another woman I really liked: Jessie Tuite, a beautiful young black girl I'd met through a friend. I remember our first conversation; I told her I was looking for my conscience and asked her if she'd seen it.

She said, "Your conscience?" and I said, "No, actually not my conscience—my heart." She said, "It's probably really small so we might want to go buy a microscope," and I said, "Come with me, we'll go buy one." I really, really liked her from the start. She was so different from most of the other drug-addled Heidi girls who were in my life then.

Things with Jessie got serious enough that Heidi and I actually split up, and in early 2002, I asked Jessie to move in with me. But she made it perfectly clear that she wouldn't even consider moving in unless I got rid of Karen, Alana, and all the other girls, and the fact that she drew that line made me like her more, so I did it. I got rid of the other women. Jessie took really good care of me. My assistant Carol sort of schooled her in what I liked, and she made sure I had things just right and ate okay and everything.

After what had happened on *Swindle*—when I'd gotten to the location only to realize I needed to have drugs sent to me if I wanted to be able to function at all—I decided to stop the meth before I did my next movie, *Dreamcatcher*. *Dreamcatcher* was this surreal horror movie Lawrence Kasdan made from a Stephen King script about four guys who end up being invaded by these parasitic aliens, and I played a military officer whom Morgan Freeman sends to lead an air strike against the aliens' ship. I didn't take any drugs with me, and I stayed sober for the shoot. I also ended up making a lifelong friend in Thomas Jane.

I liked him from day one, when we did the read-through, because he didn't have any shoes on, even though it was about one degree out. The director Lawrence Kasdan said, "Tom, did you forget to put on your shoes?" And Tom said, "I don't wear any shoes." Tom's part hillbilly. He's from the South, where you sit under the fucking willow tree and drink moonshine without your shoes on. But let me tell you, you don't want to fuck with Tom Jane because that motherfucker can fight like a goddamn animal. He's fearless.

He's also a great guy. He has a brother who has a lot of problems, and I remember he brought that brother to Paris for the *Dreamcatcher* premiere and press junket there. It was then that I saw Tom in a totally different way. He was so loving and kind and patient with his brother without ever apologizing for him. The way his brother would look at him sometimes—like he loved him more than anything in the world—was touching. Tom doesn't reveal much about himself but he's one of the brightest people I know. He's read all of Proust, all of Dostoevsky, and is a very well rounded person. He's also a self-made person, and I don't think he's even touched his abilities as an actor yet.

While we were doing *Dreamcatcher,* which was a four- or five-month undertaking, I was cast in Michael Mann's new CBS series *Robbery Homicide Division.* My character was a tough L.A. detective who went after the worst of the worst: killers, serial rapists, and white-collar criminals who were robbing poor people. It was similar, thematically, to *Heat* in that it was about an L.A. cop who was working the Robbery Homicide Division, and it was about the Los Angeles that nobody sees—where it's bloody and violent and there's no war on drugs because the drugs have won. The show was a big deal. When we went to New York for the upfronts—where the TV networks announce their new shows for the press and for advertisers who buy commercial time "up front"—Nina Tassler, who was senior vice president of drama development at CBS, said, "The casting coup for the season was getting Tom Sizemore to do *Robbery Homicide Division*." This was after *The Sopranos* had taken off and expectations were high for another phenomenal TV show.

Heidi was back in my life by then and I understood that if I was going to be able to do this TV show, I really had to stay away from the drugs. So when I knew that *Robbery Homicide Division* was definitely going to happen, I called Heidi from Canada and told her, "I've been off meth for three months and although I love you, I can't come back to that house if you're using." I told her I thought she should go to rehab but she said she didn't want to. I even told her I'd buy her a car if she went. She still didn't want to go. And though we stayed involved with each other, she felt I'd rejected her and she became even more jealous of the other women around. She was also convinced that I had stolen her little black book—the book that supposedly contained the names of all her high-profile clients and all their predilections. She convinced herself that I had taken it and hid it.

My relationship with Heidi was definitely causing problems with other people in my life as well. When I was shooting *Robbery Homicide Division,* I went to a restaurant with Heidi one night and a famous guy—I can't say who—came up to me and said, "How does it feel to be in a room where nine of the ten guys have come in your girlfriend's mouth?"

I saw her turn red when he said it, because she'd heard it—he'd said it so she could hear it. She looked stricken—like someone had stabbed her. And I'm always going to defend my girlfriend no matter what. So I grabbed him by the arm and threw him out the door of the restaurant and into the side of a car.

The cops got me out of there and called an ambulance for the guy. The two cops came to the set of *Robbery Homicide Division* the next day and basically said, "We know what happened last night and as far as we're concerned, it never happened." Michael Mann was with them, and he was very relieved. We both were. I can't tell you who it was that fixed it, but he was a very powerful friend of mine.

I'd learned from my marriage that when things start to go wrong in a relationship, there's a period when you can try to fix it, but after that point, if things still aren't working, you should get out of it. It was becoming clear that Heidi and I were both only causing each other pain, and in May 2002 I simply said to her, "I don't love you the way you love me and I think this is over." And that, combined with the fact that she assumed I had her little black book, made her incredibly angry. When she moved out, she said, "I'm going to drive you to kill yourself, motherfucker."

I didn't realize how serious she was.

The following December, Heidi's friend Brooke Ford claimed that I'd hurt her, which was not true. I always suspected that Heidi put her up to it, perhaps to lend credence to Heidi's own claims of abuse when she later filed them. But not surprisingly, Brooke didn't pursue the allegations; even though she called the cops and made the claim, she didn't show up in court, and the whole thing was dropped. But the fact that it was dropped didn't matter. What mattered was that an allegation like that was out there. The allegation is what makes news, not the fact that an allegation is dropped.

The same week that Brooke made her claim and the whole thing broke in the press, in December 2002, *Robbery Homicide Division* was canceled. It was critically acclaimed, but it just didn't have the ratings to make it. I got the news from CBS executive Les Moonves, and then, two days later, I was arrested. The show wasn't canceled because I was arrested but the personal drama I was involved in certainly didn't help anything. Still, I thought the work I was doing was some of my best yet.

Michael Mann had asked me to stay away from Heidi before I even did *Black Hawk Down,* back when we were originally talking about *Robbery Homicide Division.* But at the time, that seemed like a lot to ask. Of course, he was right and my relationship with him was entirely destroyed because of her—a true tragedy because he'd really been something of a father figure to me.

My career was really on the line. A big part of an actor's job is to stay, if not loved, at least well liked. And look, are you going to turn on the TV and watch someone you think is a piece of shit who abuses women? No, you're not.

Even though Heidi was already setting out to destroy me, she still managed to save my life one night when I had a horrible car accident in April 2003. Even though we'd broken up and she wasn't living with me anymore—and even though, by any reasonable person's logic, I should have been staying far, far away from her—Heidi and I were still meeting up. And one night after meeting up with her at a hotel, around 3:30 A.M., I turned a corner on Benedict Canyon, and I don't know who was in whose lane but there was another car there and I swerved to avoid hitting it. I wasn't intoxicated—just tired—and I was going fast. I was probably coming around that corner at 50 miles per hour, and you should be at 20. I couldn't get control of the car, and I hit the gas to get out of the way, and then I crashed into a wall. My airbag deployed and my head went through the window. It was really cold up there, and all of a sudden, I felt this warmth coming down over my face—I didn't know at the time it was blood, but that's what brought me out of the semiconscious state I was in. I saw a light in my rearview mirror; the brake light of the car that I'd avoided. I waved my arm but right after I waved, I watched the brake light go from a very bright color to a pale color and then I watched it drive away. The driver went slow for about ten feet and then raced away. They left me there to die, which leads me to believe the driver must have been drunk, because who else would do something like that?

At that time in Benedict Canyon, all the houses were way off the street and most of them were behind gates. But when I got up and dragged myself over there, I saw that there was a house with no gate. I knocked really loudly but no one answered. I was screaming, "Hey, I need help, I need help, I'm bleeding badly, I'm going to die out here!" There was no response and I could feel myself getting weaker. I went

out to the street and yelled, "Help me!" as loud as I could and then I got
to the side of the road and lay down.

That's when I checked my pockets and realized I had pot on me. Even
in that state, I was concerned about getting busted, but I could barely get
up because I'd broken my ankle and fractured my leg. Still, I managed to
get a golf club out of the trunk and use it as a cane. Blood was rolling off
my face and I looked down and saw that the white T-shirt I'd been wearing was crimson. I started to cry and said out loud, "I'm gonna die." But
I clearly didn't think so because I dug a hole with my hands, buried the
dope in there, and tried to push it down with the golf club.

Then I saw a white light from probably thirty yards away cut
through the dark and I yelled in its direction, "Help me!" It turns out
that someone was building a small complex up there in the canyon
and they had a guard shack to guard their materials. And this gentleman who was there had heard me and had gotten out a flashlight and
was walking toward me. As he got closer, the beam of his flashlight got
brighter.

This man's reaction when he saw me was so horrifying that that's
when I knew how bad I must have looked. He started to call an ambulance but I didn't think an ambulance would get me to a hospital
in enough time. I knew Heidi was just down that hill, so I used his cell
phone to call her. She got right up there and put me in her car and
then she called her dad, who's a doctor, and asked him to recommend
a surgeon.

When we got to Century City Hospital, the surgeon came in and
said, "We're going to fix this—I'm the Michael Jordan of surgery. And
you're going to have to be the Michael Jordan of patients because I
can't give you any anesthetic at all—there's too much glass in this cut.
You have to be completely awake and with me." I was crying and he
said, "You have to stop crying, goddamn it. Otherwise, you're going

to have a big gash on your forehead. Is that what you want?" He was tough on me, but I respond well to extreme pressure.

The surgery was nineteen hours long and it took three weeks for me to recuperate. I was making a movie called *Paparazzi* at the time and they had to shut down production for two weeks and then work around me for the week after. For those few weeks, I looked like Frankenstein, and when I healed and got back to work, I thought I'd survived the biggest ordeal of my life. I had no idea that the true ordeal was just about to hit.

PAPARAZZI HAD BEEN back in production for another three weeks when Mel Gibson, who was producing the movie, walked up to me one day on set.

"You're about to be arrested," he said. I asked for what and he said, "Heidi said you hit her." I was sure he was kidding—I almost started to laugh—but I looked into his eyes and saw that he was entirely serious. A series of incidents flashed before me: different fights Heidi and I had gotten into, her threat that she would destroy my life, but also memories of how loving and supportive she'd been the night of my accident and so many other times. Even though I wasn't high, in many ways I felt like I was: everything took on a veil of surreality. And I thought, "Well, this is all a misunderstanding. I'll just clear this up— whatever it is—and maybe even laugh about it later." But while the veil of surreality lasted, nothing ever got cleared up. Before I could even say anything to Mel, the cops were standing there in front of me. I guess they'd gone to my house first and my housekeeper had told them I was at work. They told me that they'd let me finish my day on the set but that I'd need to turn myself in later that evening.

I went into my work mode—where I just focused on my lines and dove into the character I was playing as much as I possibly could, while telling myself not to react until I had all of the facts. I called my attorney—someone CAA had recommended, named Michael Fitzgerald—and after work, he came and picked me up and took me to a Taco Bell parking lot nearby where the cops were waiting. I was booked and after I bailed out, Michael drove me home.

My relationship with Heidi had been passionate from the beginning: everything we did together was in extremes, from the drugs to the love to the eventual hatred. And because meth imbued so much of our relationship, everything was exacerbated and heightened. When we were angry, we both said a lot of things we didn't mean and left each other angry messages when we were fighting. But I had never hit her and I assumed the truth would come out quickly or that she would drop her case. Heidi would not let that happen, however; she was determined to make me pay.

I didn't call Heidi right away. It was only three weeks after she'd saved my life, and I was really in too much shock to talk to her. I could barely talk to anyone. The Brooke Ford accusation had been one thing—a claim by a random girl that was dropped. But Heidi had been deeply embedded in my world, had been someone I truly loved, and this was the deepest betrayal possible. Though part of me clung to this idea that the truth would come out and the whole mess would be over, another part of me knew that when Heidi set her mind to something, she didn't let go. In a certain way, I understood that life as I knew it was over.

CHAPTER 6

FULL-COURT PRESS

AS THE SUMMER of 2003 chugged along, Heidi added more fuel to her fire. I called to talk to her about her accusations and we ended up getting in another fight; she reported what I'd said during the conversation, labeling it witness intimidation, and I was arrested again. I began to realize that Heidi wasn't just out to get revenge on *me*: she wanted to make me pay for every wrong that had ever been committed against her by anyone.

But I knew that I was telling the truth and so I went into the trial that August confident that her lies would be exposed. The trial is a bit of a blur. I just sat there for the eleven days, despondent over what my life had become. I was advised not to take the stand, and I didn't. Heidi testified for three days, crying and saying that I'd left her ninety harassing phone calls and had beat her.

Most of the focus was on April 8, 2002, a night when Tom Jane was over at my house because I was showing him the pilot of a film Michael Madsen and I were putting together. The *National Enquirer* had run some story saying that I was sleeping with other women—something Heidi knew about already—and she was pissed. We'd already fought about it. That night she called and started in about that again. We were arguing over the phone about it but clearly weren't getting anywhere, so when I hung up, I disconnected the phone. That's when she showed up, completely irate. We went outside and kept arguing while Tom Jane tried to intervene and get us to stop. I'm not going to lie—I was angry. I told her to give back the Porsche I'd given her as a gift and I wasn't too gracious about it. And that upset her so much that when I headed back inside, she jumped on me and bit my ear. I flinched and she went flying off my back, falling onto the driveway. She claimed that I *threw* her onto the driveway, which was patently untrue. The truth is that she was completely out of control and I just wanted her out of my house. Tom tried to help as best as he could, giving her ice and ultimately driving her to her sister's house. And during the trial, Tom explained all of that; he was out of town so he gave his testimony over video.

Heidi also claimed that I'd put a cigarette out on her and beat her at the Four Seasons Hotel in New York because she'd criticized *Black Hawk Down* on Howard Stern—despite the fact that there were no witnesses or medical records from this alleged incident. She also claimed that I'd punched her in the jaw at the Beverly Hills Hotel on April 8, which was literally five nights before she saved my life after my car accident. She said all sorts of ridiculous things. She claimed we had a contract that said that I'd pay her half a million dollars if I hit her. She also claimed that I destroyed her collection of china figurines with a baseball bat and threatened to kill her brother.

I was guilty—guilty of losing my temper and leaving her horrible messages both when we were in our fights and when I called to talk to her about her accusations. I heard every single one of those messages during the trial because they played them in court. And I felt terrible—terrible when I left them and even more terrible when I heard them. The things I said were, without question, wrong. Heidi and I had a really twisted, drug-fueled, dysfunctional relationship, and the way we talked to each other was hardly delicate, but that didn't give me license to say the things that I did.

There were a great many holes in Heidi's testimony, but I was so far gone on the drugs at that point that I wasn't able to focus on it. In fact, we were later able to argue that the pictures she presented as evidence were phony. In my petition for a writ of habeas corpus, a photo expert named Jeffrey Sedlik concluded that. Heidi had claimed a friend of hers named Tara Dabrizzi had shot the main photo being used as evidence and that the reason nobody could find this girl—because believe me, I tried—was that she'd left the country the next day. I knew that if we could prove that Heidi had taken the photo herself, we would be able to overturn my conviction.

I finally concluded that Tara Dabrizzi either was a fictional person or she was born in her home and essentially never left it—never having had a birth certificate, hospital record, Social Security number, driver's license, health insurance, W-2, or utility bill—except for the day Heidi claimed the photos were taken that she presented in court as proof of my guilt, and never surfaced again. These were photos that irrevocably, drastically transformed my life and yet the fact that Dabrizzi probably didn't actually exist never came up in my trial.

In the habeas corpus filing, Sedlik said that you could see it was Heidi taking the picture of herself—something that was obvious once you looked at the photo closely. He also said that the focus pattern was "an optical impossibility" because the bruise was in soft focus while other parts of the photo, such as her hair and chin, were in sharp focus.

Nothing about what Heidi claimed during the trial made sense to me, and yet she was never really questioned on any of it. She claimed that I had punched her twice, but the photos she presented as evidence showed only one possible injury. And the day after the attack supposedly took place, Heidi spent the night with me at the Bel Air Hotel, which doesn't make any sense if she was really, as she claimed, feeling like her life was in danger around me. Another thing that Sedlik figured out from examining the camera's metadata is that the photos weren't taken on April 13, which Heidi claimed was a few days after the supposed attack took place, but on May 12. Heidi was amazing with computers and photos and yet none of this was ever examined. And we're talking about the testimony of someone who had been convicted of nine felonies.

Much later, in July 2007, another lawyer I hired ended up interviewing Dr. Michael Carden, the plastic surgeon who'd stitched me up the night of the car accident. Carden explained that Heidi didn't have any bruises or any sign of injuries when he treated me, and that we clearly got along well. For the appeals that followed, I went through a slew of other attorneys. I essentially spent millions on these lawyers at a time when I wasn't raking in millions anymore.

Heidi convinced everyone. She sobbed on the witness stand and claimed that the reason she didn't file charges at the time was that she was afraid no one would believe her. The jury, which was made up of seven men and five women, deliberated for three days. On August 18, they threw out most of the claims and I was found guilty of one count each of domestic violence, criminal threats, vandalism, and harassing phone calls. The domestic violence charge was for the incident she claimed happened at the Beverly Hills Hotel, a few days before the car accident when she saved me.

My bail was set at one hundred thousand dollars and I was told that I was facing up to four years in prison, but that the sentencing would happen when we returned to court in October.

Even though I knew it could have gone worse, I was still devastated. But I did everything I could not to show that: after getting the news, the only statement I gave was one thanking my family and fans for their support.

SHORTLY AFTER THE trial, I made a movie called *Hustle,* in which I played Pete Rose—the former major-league baseball player and manager who was busted for betting on baseball when he was playing for and managing the Cincinnati Reds. It was the first opportunity I had to work with the great Peter Bogdanovich, and there was quite a lot about Rose's life that I related to. Playing a guy who had once received great accolades before having the press and then the world turn against him came pretty naturally to me.

Peter Bogdanovich and I worked well together. He told me that he thought I was extremely creative in terms of my ideas for blocking and movement and he was never afraid to say, "Actually, that's a little quirky" and suggest I do something else. And I think in large part because of our relationship, I managed to stay sober for the entirety of the twenty-day shoot.

Peter would tell me that I really got "under the skin of the character" and found Pete Rose within me, rather than doing it in what he called Paul Muni style. Muni was a 1930s actor known for immersing himself in the study of the traits and mannerisms of the real person being portrayed. Peter would say that people have a mistaken understanding of acting because they think it's about being somebody else when you can't actually *be* somebody else; so it's really about how to best "look for the character in you" and find the facet of them that you can identify with. He told me that all the greats—Cary Grant, John Wayne, Jimmy Stewart, any of those guys—acted that way.

Even though a lot of directors might have considered me a liability at that point in time, Peter doesn't really care about that kind of thing. He used to say that Mary McBride Smith, John Ford's wife, would tell him, "Pete, if you want to stay in the movie business, never believe everything you hear and only believe half of what you see." So he said he never listened to anything anyone else said about actors. Peter was just generally not judgmental. He saw more actors on coke in the 1970s and '80s than probably anyone else, and when he talked to me about drugs, all he said was "You know, you should be careful."

By then, I'd worked with a variety of creative geniuses who were often a bit cantankerous, and I actually felt that the animosity between us could summon up more interesting performances out of me. So sometimes I'd want to stir things up with Peter. But he just wouldn't bite. I'd say to him, "Why don't you do something to make me hate you? I can't work with directors I don't hate. Do something hateful." And he'd just respond, "Tom, you're crazy." At one point I asked him, "Aren't you ever a prick?" And he said, "I'm just not." He kept a friendly, upbeat feeling on set.

We did get into a beef one time when we had to finish a scene in very little time and I was complaining about it. He suddenly snapped at me, "What the hell do you want to do about it?" I'm actually incredibly sensitive and get my feelings hurt fairly easily, which always seems to surprise people. I was pretty taken aback and just sort of walked away, but he followed after me and we patched things up quickly.

Peter told me that his favorite scene in the movie is one near the end, where I'm being interrogated and I definitely say that I never bet on baseball. He said that the brilliance of it was that you somehow believed me even though you knew I was lying because you'd actually seen me bet. The irony, of course, was that I'd just been in court telling the truth while everyone assumed I was lying.

But aside from brief moments of being able to work with people like Peter Bogdanovich, my life just continued to go downhill. And one day when I was feeling incredibly frustrated by the state my life was in, I called my manager, Beth, and asked if she could come over. I wanted to see if there was some way she could help me get out of all the trouble I was in, but we ended up having a massive fight, which resulted in the dissolution of our relationship. We did work together again, briefly, when Rob Lowe helped me get on his show *Dr. Vegas*, but our relationship was never really the same.

The drugs had really lost their joie de vivre for me, as had life. I remember waking up one morning and saying to myself, "Why bother?" I was chained to that fucking pipe and I had this kind of deflated feeling where all the air had left my body and I felt like a bag of bones. It was a monumental effort just to get out of bed. On the one hand, I'd feel okay whenever I got more dope because I'd say to myself, "Hey, I've got a couple million dollars and everything is groovy," but at the same time, I knew things were the opposite of groovy and that what I was doing was really, really wrong. I'd sit there on the couch and ask myself what I was doing but also feel like I had no choice but to keep hitting the pipe. And then I'd think or say out loud, "I'm going to stop," and the next second I'd take another hit off the pipe. And then I'd think, "Okay, I'm going to call rehabs as soon as I finish everything I have." And then I'd call rehabs—I'd call places in Israel or Finland and ask them if they had any beds. They'd say, "Yes, where are you calling from?" and I'd answer, "L.A." There would be a pause and then the person would say, "Well, sir, they have many rehabilitation centers in L.A.—maybe you should check there first." I'd hang up the phone, knowing that I wasn't really ready to change or else why the fuck would I have been calling a rehab in Finland? So then I'd throw myself into something like reading Proust.

After enough nights like this, I essentially fell into a monumental depression that no drug could ever remedy or make me forget. I couldn't do much of anything. And whenever I'd start to feel better, I'd see a headline about "Tom Sizemore, the woman batterer" and sink again.

So one night near when I was due back in court, I'd just had it. I took somewhere in the neighborhood of two hundred—I think it was 182—of my antidepressant trazodone, put on the song "Motion Picture Soundtrack" by Radiohead, turned the lights off in my house, and lay down in my gym. I really believed I was lying down to die. I was so fucked-up during that period of time that I'd forgotten that suicide was a permanent solution to a temporary problem.

Jessie, the UCLA student that I'd been seeing, just happened to stop by. She wasn't living with me at the time but I think she had a bad feeling about something so she took a cab up there. And when the cab pulled through the gate and she saw that all the lights were off, she knew something was wrong and she ran in screaming my name. I was unconscious, so I didn't hear it, but that's what she told me afterward.

She somehow knew to run to the gym—that was an area of my house that was just mine, that none of the girls or anyone else used—and found me back there, passed out, lying flat on my back with a glass of water and six empty pill bottles next to me. She told me later that my face was already blue, so she raced outside and stopped the cabdriver, already halfway down the driveway, and got him to turn around and come back.

Initially he was telling her "I don't want to be part of this," but she convinced him to take us by assuring him that he didn't have to be a part of anything and could just drop us off at a hospital. And so he drove us to Sherman Oaks Hospital, where they rolled me out of the cab. All I knew is that when I came to, I had a catheter up my dick. I cried for five hours when they told me how close I was to death, and I wasn't surprised that they decided to keep me in the 5150 wing for a few days.

I went back to court in late October. People showed up to support me. Charlie Sheen and a few other friends were there. I was definitely humbled by everything that had happened, and I'd written a letter to that effect, which was read in court. The judge concluded that my problem was drug addiction and sentenced me to six months in jail, but he said that I could get my sentence cut in half if I successfully completed rehab.

So I went to a rehab called Rancho L'Abri in Mexico. Once again, I thought I wanted to get clean. But the drugs had a serious hold of me at this point—even more than they did before, because now I really wanted to blot out reality with a vengeance. They didn't work anymore—I got no relief from them whatsoever—but I had to use them all the time to feel okay. Which is why I brought speed into rehab with me on some paper in a notebook.

The first night I was there, I did the speed. I'd figured out after Heidi had slipped the speed in my Visine bottle how to transport speed myself and discovered that you could put it on a piece of paper and then put a few drops of distilled water on it. If you use regular water, the chemicals ruin the speed, but distilled water doesn't have all this shit in it, so it's fine. The speed is actually contained on there, very concentrated. You can't go into a rehab or through airport security with seventy-five pieces of torn paper, but you can have a couple of phone numbers in your pocket, maybe one in your wallet, and another in your notebook, and that's all you need. That's two thousand dollars' worth of speed. And if you're not in a situation where you can take it out when you want to do the drugs, you can always just eat it. It's not good for your stomach or your teeth, but it works. And nobody searching your bag is going to be suspicious of a few pieces of paper scattered around.

Rancho L'Abri wasn't a lockdown rehab but it was a serious motherfucker, so they had security at night patrolling the fence and whole area. To even get to the fence was hard. And I'd decided I wanted out.

Later that first night—on November 22, 2003—I went to bed just after midnight. But at around three in the morning, I got up, did more speed, and pulled my blanket around me. I walked down the hall and, as I passed a tech, I muttered, "Fuck, man, any dope in this fucking place?" as if I was in pain, but I was actually high as a kite. I'd brought a mister bottle with me and had misted my face so it looked like I was sweating out a detox.

I went outside to smoke a cigarette. I watched the fence, counting how long it took the guard to get from one point to the next; it was a couple of minutes. Sometimes it was ten minutes, but you have to plan for the shortest amount of time. I was forty-one years old, and I knew that getting over that fence was going to be hard. I felt like Paul Newman in *Cool Hand Luke*.

I managed to climb over the fence and then walk the nine miles to the freeway and to a waiting limousine that I'd called and ordered from L.A. One of the girls who was living in my house was in the car, and we got high and had sex on the way back. The only way I can explain why I did what I did is that my addiction was like a beast at that point and the beast was running the show.

When I woke up the next morning and remembered what I'd done, I almost had a heart attack. I thought I was going to prison. I called Rose, the administrator at Rancho L'Abri, and she said, "Get back here right away." So I went back. And then, three days later, I did the same thing: climbed the fence, called the driver, walked the nine miles, and went all the way home to Benedict Canyon. But this time when I called, Rose said, "If you leave again, you can't come back and you're going to go to prison."

So then I went back and stayed. I grew to like it there. Rose was very fair and a really nice lady. It was my favorite treatment center: I just liked the way it looked and I liked the instructors. It was beautiful and everyone who worked there was a recovering addict. I don't like many treatment centers, but they were really smart people there. They were all little Bob Forrests: very eccentric, smart, fun to be with. These people were having fun, so they actually made rehab fun. Of course, it still didn't make a difference for my recovery because I was a hope-to-die addict by then.

I was only supposed to stay forty-five days but I actually stayed fifty-seven. But after I was released, I got high yet again. I'd learned nothing. I still had money and I was an arrogant fool. And I didn't realize how altered my reasoning had become.

All I had to do was go to a sober-living house for ten and a half months and I'd have been off probation and nothing else would have happened to me. Everybody who cared about me—my rehab counselor, my father, Bob Forrest—told me to leave rehab and go straight to sober living. Bob said, "If you want to get high, get high after your probation's over." Bob believes in harm reduction. His philosophy is let's get the person out of trouble and then let him deal with the addiction.

So I listened to all these really smart people but ignored all of them because my reasoning was so skewed by the meth and all the sex I was having. But it was really the meth way more than it was the sex. When it came down to it, I'd have preferred the drugs to the girls, hands down. I don't like thinking of myself as someone who would choose an inanimate object over a human being, but that's the God's honest truth.

The thing is, I knew I was going to get high when I was still in rehab. I'd gone online, googled "ways to beat urine tests when on probation in California," and found out about this device called the Whizzinator, which is a fake penis that comes with dried urine, a syringe, and heater packs to keep the urine at body temperature. I ordered one and had it shipped to my house. But because the girls who were living at my house weren't the smartest and I was afraid one of them might intercept and then lose the package, I had two more shipped there.

Without something like a Whizzinator, beating drug tests is actually really hard. It used to be that if you didn't get high for twelve hours, then drank enough water and took these capsules called Urine Luck for four hours before, you tested clean. But probation officers started to figure out that people were flushing drugs out of their system with water, so they made a rule that your urine wouldn't count if it contained over a certain percentage of water.

What you have to go through if you're using and want to pass a test is horrific. I did it once, but I could never go through it again. For four days, I sat in a steam room all day, drinking water and not eating, and then I spent a day drinking this disgusting thing they make gelatin with. Then, the day before the test, I drank half a bottle of vinegar so I'd throw up. I then drank cranberry juice with water before taking seven aspirin. It was insane, and the whole time I was doing it, I wanted to die. Your stomach is distended from the water so you're pissing all the time. For it to really work, you're supposed to be able to take nine pisses an hour. Do you know how much water you have to put in your body to piss that often? And we're talking about a body that's already fucked-up from drugs, so it's not working right anyway, and it's not used to having fluids in it because most drug addicts are not drinking enough water.

If you have enough money, you can actually inject clear piss into your bladder. It's not healthy but it's a quick fix and you piss it out in two hours. I didn't do that, but I've heard that some guys in the NFL do.

So I started using the Whizzinator and fake piss—synthetic urine—a lot. Now, if any probation officer or observer of a urine test were to look closely at anyone using the Whizzinator, they'd see it wasn't real. But the rationale when you're getting tested is that the people who are testing you look at dicks all day long so the last thing they want to do is look at another person's dick, much less when they're pissing. I overheard one probation officer say, "I've been here eighteen years; you don't want to know how many dicks I've seen piss." They all feel like that on some level. Nobody wants to look at three hundred dicks a day peeing in a cup. And let's be honest: these are probably not the nicest dicks. We're talking about people just out of prison who probably don't have the best hygiene.

Once you take your dick out, they're going to look away if they assume you're clean. And once I understood that beating the test was really all about acting casual so that they didn't feel like they even had to watch me pee, I realized that how I behaved once I walked in the door was more important than anything else. If I came into the room and the prevailing wisdom was that I was not using drugs, the PO wouldn't even look, really. I went through a long period of time where I was using drugs, but I'd stop using them as much when I had to get tested. I'd do my best to look good. I'd get a haircut and a facial, and try in general to look as much like a movie star as I could. Then I'd go in there with a Visine bottle to hold under my testicles or the Whizzinator. The PO would hand me the bottle and say, "Sizemore, what's going on, man?" I'd say, "Not much, man," and then he'd stand across the room while I was at the urinal because I would have convinced him, through the way I looked and the way I was behaving, that I was clean. But you can only do that in the beginning of using—when you're out of rehab and for about nine months afterward. Eventually the drug tears you down so much that it doesn't matter how many tanning salons you go to; you just can't look good when you've lost twenty-eight pounds and there's wear and tear on your face from being awake all the time. You can't turn the clock back unless you go to rehab.

My problems kept piling up while I was in this phase of using drugs and getting tested. I tested dirty in March 2004 and was refused a new trial in July. The judge just didn't understand why, since I got caught with my hand in the cookie jar and my whole life changed, I'd go and put my hand in there again. He would say, "Approach the bench, Mr. Sizemore," and when I did, he'd say, "What is wrong with you, what do you need? Do you want to come up here and I'll play golf with you once a week?"

He saw a guy with obvious good qualities—talent, good things in his life before, college-educated. He'd say, "You're ruining your life with this drug. Don't you know you're doing that and that it's going to leave me no choice but to put you in prison again?" I have to imagine that it's impossible for someone who wasn't as bad an addict as I was to even understand this, but I *did* know that I was ruining my life, and I was so far gone that I couldn't seem to be able to do anything to stop it. Once he realized I was hopelessly addicted and not just a bad person, he became different. Initially he was just angry with me. But he took on a fatherly role after a while.

At this point, cops were showing up at my house regularly. There were people partying and being loud and playing music, and the neighbors would call. Those cops would always try to freak me out, but I considered them Keystone Kops and called them that.

All I could do for a long time was just try to stay positive and tell myself that things would work themselves out, but at the same time, I didn't believe in myself. I'd wanted to stop doing drugs but hadn't been able to so many times, and I'd made so many terrible decisions that I doubted myself. I'd never really doubted myself before. A lot of my drug taking was to obscure that, I think.

One night in August of 2004, I had some people over and the cops showed up at my house at about six in the morning. I had asked Jessie to hide the meth I had, and she put it in a bag somewhere, but they searched the whole house, found it, and arrested me. At the time, I blamed Jessie but the truth is, it was all my fault—it was my meth. I went to court for that in October and was given thirty-six months of probation. All I had to do was be good. But I didn't know if that was possible.

I'VE EXPERIENCED MY fair share of dramatic phone calls in my life, but none was more dramatic than the one I got in December 2004 from Jinele McIntire, a woman I'd been with for a total of nine days and had sex with maybe four times. She told me she was pregnant. Jinele was a pretty brunette from a middle-class family in Palm Springs who went to Palm Springs High School, and that was literally about all I knew about her when we got together. I met her through Slash, the guitarist from Guns N' Roses, whom I knew through his wife, Perla Hudson, who was an old friend of Heidi's. It was as simple as this: one day I went to see Slash, I started talking to an attractive woman who was over there, things got amorous—and suddenly I was going to be a dad.

She didn't say what she wanted to do and I told her that I'd support whatever she decided, but I also let her know that I was in much bigger trouble than she might realize. This was right around the time that my business manager had told me I was broke. I'd spent over $10 million on legal fees and wasn't raking in the dough the way I once had, but I hadn't known that I was even close to broke. He had wanted to spare me the stress of the situation, but suddenly he was telling me that I had to sell my house or else the bank was going to foreclose on it. It was heartbreaking and, honestly, I didn't care about money until I lost it, which makes me wish sometimes that I'd never had it at all.

In February of 2005, I went back to court, where the judge told me he thought I was out of control. He was right. He said, "There are two ways for you to go: one is to recover and the other is to die." Unfortunately, I didn't feel ready to recover yet. The next month, I officially filed for bankruptcy and lost my house. I tried to face the world—I did an interview on *Dateline*—but it was all so upsetting that I got angry in the middle of the interview and stormed off, though I came back and apologized. In May I was ordered back to court again because I hadn't given my probation officer my new address, then I went back to court in June and stupidly denied faking the drug tests. I missed my next hearing, and then it was back to rehab again.

The next month, Jinele gave birth to our twin sons, Jayden and Jagger. I wanted to be able to provide for my kids, but I wasn't exactly being offered *Heat* or *Saving Private Ryan* anymore. I did a small movie called *Splinter* with Edward James Olmos and another one called *Shut Up and Shoot!* with Daniel Baldwin and Gary Busey. Like I said, not *Saving Private Ryan*.

Then, that September, I got busted faking a drug test with the Whizzinator. I had the Whizzinator sewn together between two pairs of underwear. You really couldn't see a thing, and I'd been getting away with this forever. But the PO who was in there with me knew that I was intoxicated. I'd gotten to the point where I couldn't really hide it anymore.

Obviously, this kind of ridiculous thing makes news. Howard Stern called me and said, "I hear your cock's really popular in Hollywood." I told him, "Call the DA; he's got it now." But all jokes aside, I was humiliated. And screwed. Which is a terrible combination.

In October, instead of putting me in prison, they reinstated my probation. I was grateful that I wasn't being put away, but at the same time, I didn't think things could get much worse.

CHAPTER 7

THE DARKNESS BEFORE THE DAWN

ON NOVEMBER 1, 2005, I officially didn't have anywhere to live anymore—I couldn't even afford a small apartment—and I was still with Jessie, so we moved into a sober-living house in Whittier. Because I was so out of it, I didn't actually understand how Prop 36 worked. If I'd understood it, I could have had the government pay for it, but I didn't so instead my mom did.

I was a guy who'd come from very little and risen to the top: I'd had the multimillion-dollar house, the Porsche, the restaurant I partially owned with Robert De Niro. And now I had absolutely nothing. I had about eleven dollars in my pocket. Even though I've never cared all that much about money, to have sunk lower than where I started out truly decimated me.

By this point, Jessie and I were both doing a lot of meth, even though it was making us miserable—and even though we were staying in a sober-living place. I was so hooked on meth by then that I was convinced I could never get off of it. There's a reason that meth is public enemy number one: it fucks up your judgment. I never did anything as outrageous as some other people I've heard about—I never thought I was talking to God or jumped off the roof of a building because I believed I was Jesus—but I felt those kinds of thoughts coming on. And of course I wouldn't have been homeless if my judgment hadn't been completely fucked. There's something about meth that's different than other drugs: doing it after a while just feels completely unnatural and wrong. The high is so intense that it makes your thoughts go to dark places and after a while you're seeing distorted figures and shadow people and nothing but horror around you.

We stayed in Whittier until the following May, when I was able to rent an apartment in the San Fernando Valley with the money I'd made on a couple of straight-to-video movies. But I owed a lot of people at that point, so after paying them back, I had trouble continuing to make my rent on my place in the Valley. After three months, I gave up on that and moved into a friend's garage in Studio City.

Jessie and I had already been videotaping a lot of stuff, and that's when I decided to start documenting my own downfall—what ended up becoming *Shooting Sizemore,* a piece-of-shit reality show that aired on VH1. The whole idea, when I sold it to the production company, was that my footage was going to carry the day, but there was less than one percent of my footage in there and the only stuff they used is really ugly—just me smoking speed and carrying a fake gun around, completely out of context.

But with the advance I made on *Shooting Sizemore,* I got a loft downtown and Jessie and I moved in there. I managed to put some sober days together, but then I slipped again. This was a period when I overdosed a lot. I'd be with people shooting dope and then all of a sudden, I'd fall over. They'd take me to Cedars-Sinai and push me out the door of the car. They didn't want to call EMS because they didn't want to get arrested, and they didn't want to be charged with murder if I died, so they'd just take me to the ER and leave me there. I can't say I blame them.

The first time it happened, I had to be told that I had OD'd, but after that, whenever I'd wake up in the hospital, I'd understand the situation right away, pull the IV out of my arm, and say, "I didn't die so I'm going home." I'd ignore the doctors and walk outside, where I would call up the people I'd been using with and say, "What happened, where's my fucking dope and where's my car? One of you come over here and get me." After about six months of this, I went into Cri-Help, a no-frills rehab in North Hollywood. I stayed at Cri-Help from the beginning of April through July, when I went to Canada to do a movie called *Superstorm.*

By then, I'd met a pornographer guy who owned property out in Sylmar, which is about a half hour outside Los Angeles. Sylmar is best known as the town where Charles Manson hid Rosemary LaBianca's wallet after killing her, in the hope that someone would find the wallet, use the credit cards, and be framed for the murder. And, well, that just about sums up how creepy a place it was. It was a place where fine dining meant Shakey's Pizza Parlor or Casa Torres for Mexican. It's a bunch of unpaved dirt roads and overgrown fields of tumbleweed. Olive trees that once flourished—once upon a time, before World War II, Sylmar-brand olives were sold all over the United States—now dotted dusty lanes through a landscape of deserted barns and sheds.

After *Superstorm,* Jessie and I moved into one of those places. It was, ostensibly, a cabin on this guy's property, but I think that's doing the word *cabin* a disservice. It had no electricity, running water, ventilation, or even doorknobs. It was an abandoned shithole, and the door didn't close all the way, so dirt blew in, though I did fix it up by painting it and rigging up the electricity. Yes, my life had sunk so low that it was a big thrill when I was able to steal electricity from someone living nearby who had actually paid for it. Being homeless might have been better because at least when you're completely homeless, the chance always exists that you can go stay with someone in a nice place.

At this point, I was continuing to do the meth not just because I was hopelessly addicted but also so that I could block everything out as much as possible. I was as lost as I've ever been. The best thing I can say about that time in my life, though, is that the cops couldn't raid me anymore because no one knew where we were. Still, the only sign of civilization was a 7-Eleven about eight miles away—that was our Statue of Liberty—and the guy who owned the property we were on filmed porn all the time, so you'd wake up in the morning and see people out on the balcony having sex.

Before long, this pornographer guy started talking to me about doing a sex tape, and I was so desperate for fucking money—so desperate in general—that I listened to him. So one evening I had sex with six girls that he picked out for me. It was disgusting, disturbing, and shows you what methamphetamine does to your judgment. Honestly, out of all the ridiculous things I did, that's the one I most want to take back.

I checked back into rehab—at Las Encinas this time—and put together some more sober time. Then, in January 2007, I met with a casting director I'd known for a long time, Mary Vernieu, about doing a movie called *American Son,* which was shooting in Bakersfield— about a hundred miles north of Los Angeles. Mary asked me point blank if I was sober, and I lied to her and said yes, even though I was in the midst of a full-blown relapse. Because I was only about a month into using really heavily, the wear and tear hadn't started in any kind of an outwardly noticeable way. But I was smoking a lot of meth every day and I swore up and down that I wasn't. And by the time I needed to work on the movie in April, I was only in worse shape.

I worked for two weeks and then, three and a half weeks later, I had to go back to shoot just one more scene. Now, during the two weeks that I'd been on the movie before, I'd stayed at the Four Points Sheraton in Bakersfield. I'd been relatively quiet during that time because I was working, but one of my using buddies who was working as my assistant on the movie was not. I got him a room in the same hotel on a different floor. I had met a girl up there and, unbeknownst to me, he had gotten friendly with her and made this arrangement that he would sell dope to her and her friends. So he was having his wife FedEx drugs to him there at the hotel, and he was selling it to these people, which means there were a lot of people coming and going at all hours. I didn't know about any of this, but I guess the hotel got tired of what was going on, and since his room was in my name, they banned me from the hotel. But we didn't know any of that yet.

My friend drove me to Bakersfield the day I had that one scene, and the plan was for me to just go to the set, do my one scene, and come right back. But he kept saying we should check back into the hotel and stay the night. I had no idea that it was so he could have a place to sell a bunch of dope to the people he'd met there. When we got to Bakersfield, he pulled up at the hotel. I asked him what he was doing and he told me that he had an outstanding bill there that he had to take care of—that the hotel had charged him for a blanket when we'd stayed there the month before and he needed to pay for it. I told him I'd wait in the car.

So he walked into the hotel and said he needed a room under the name Tom Sizemore. The guy at the front desk said, "There's no room here for him." My friend was high and pissed. He snapped, "Yes there is—check your fucking records!" And the guy responded, "I don't need to check my records. I'm the one that banned him from this hotel." My friend still wasn't getting it, and told the guy to go get his boss. This gentleman at the front desk had a harelip so my friend added, "You know that harelip you have? You're about to get another one if you don't go get him now." The guy excused himself, and my friend thought that his threats had scared the guy into going to get his boss. So my friend, who was on parole, stood there for eighteen full minutes—with a pipe, enough meth to get high with, and Klonopin pills in his pocket—while I was outside in the car, asleep. I'd been reading the paper and had fallen asleep with the *USA Today* sports page on my chest. What my friend didn't know is that what he'd said to the guy counted as a terrorist threat, and so the guy had called the cops.

The cops came, searched my friend, found his pipe, and handcuffed him. I didn't have long to go before my probation was up, and I would have walked away from all my legal troubles—I was telling myself, in fact, that I was only partying so much because I was celebrating how close I was to freedom. But for reasons I still can't explain but that my former friend may know, somehow the cops decided to come outside and search the car. The cops came out, and I woke up to a bunch of them standing there pointing guns at me, with one of them saying, "Show me your hands."

They searched me and they searched the car and when they found the meth, they asked me whose it was. I said, "Not mine." He and I were both arrested and taken to jail in Bakersfield in separate cars. I bailed out and went to stay with a woman who was working as my agent at the time.

When I went to court on May 8, people showed up for me. My mother had seen Martin Sheen on TV talking about how horrible it was that the California's Drug Court focused on punishment rather than recovery from addiction and she called up his agent to ask him to come to court with me. He spoke at length with my mother on the phone, and then not only took his seat in court, right there next to my brother Paul, but also spoke to the press afterward, saying that he didn't think prison was appropriate for someone in the grips of drug and alcohol abuse.

Of course, in the end, his kindness didn't matter. On May 22, I was charged with five felonies and one misdemeanor and had another hearing set for June 5. My request for bail was denied on June 6, so I was taken to L.A. County Jail. After all the close calls, it was really happening now: with only two and a half weeks to go on my probation, I had been completely busted and was going to prison. My probation officer, who had been my PO for four years, actually cried. I was put in HPPC, or "high-powered protective custody"—where you go if you're famous. There you're kept separate all the time.

I stayed in jail until June 26, when I went back to court, and that's when I was sentenced to sixteen months in prison for probation violation. Sixteen motherfucking months. The next day brought the only bit of good news during that entire period: my sentence was cut in half because of the time I'd already spent behind bars and at rehabs. But I couldn't believe it: I'd survived the Fleiss ordeal but was going to prison anyway because of meth.

Because there was another actor in Chino State Prison at the time—Lane Garrison, who was on the TV show *Prison Break* and was convicted of vehicular manslaughter for killing two kids in a drunk-driving accident—I was moved from there to Delano State Prison in Kern County. Inmates want to either kill or extort actors who are in prison—there's no HPPC there—and I guess they just didn't think it was a good idea to have both of us.

I was transferred to Delano on August 2. My experiences in both places were horrific but the Kern County facility was especially run-down; it was a horrendous, awful, filthy place. I have to say, prison was even worse than I'd feared it would be and I feared it was going to be pretty bad. I'd honestly rather be dead than go back there for a week.

I was in solitary confinement initially. That's the California penal system's version of protective custody. It's called 1750, and it's where O. J. Simpson and Robert Downey were. But their version of protective custody was to put me in the hole. Usually the hole is for people who have misbehaved—either killed somebody or been caught with narcotics—but that's where I went.

When I was out of solitary, this is what it was like: I'd wake up on a bed that was made out of round wires, where'd I'd been sleeping on a shitty mattress that was from Goodwill in probably the 1900s. The intercom noise that blared at six in the morning was the loudest, most jarring sound you could possibly imagine, so every morning my goal was to wake up before that: getting up was bad enough without it. So I'd get out of bed and wait for my cell door to open, at which point I'd walk down to the chow hall with the other guys.

The time you ate depended on the section of the prison you were in: first cell block A went, then B, then C. They stacked it like that because it cut down on the number of fights that broke out. You're heavily guarded the whole time you're eating. Breakfast would be a lot of potatoes and scrambled eggs and these really unpleasant pancakes, and then you'd pick up your lunch in a bag for later: peanut butter and jelly and some old fruit. And you'd go back to chow for dinner.

There's really no way to describe what being in prison is like to someone who hasn't lived it. All you're thinking about all the time is how you can avoid getting hurt. And you try to make sense of the fact that this, for the moment, is your home, and yet you're surrounded by barbed wire. I would sit there and think, "Man, I was just a couple of mistakes away from glory." Because I felt like I was close to glory when I was starring in major motion pictures. And let me tell you, when you're in prison, the word *glory* doesn't enter your mind—it isn't even a part of your vocabulary anymore.

To get through the days, I would try to reenact all of the plays I'd done in college, graduate school, and New York and also recite dialogue from my favorite film roles. I initially just wanted to make sure my memory was still intact after all the drug abuse. But after a while, I just did it to pass the time. Later, I wrote to my mom and asked her to send me books; I remember that I asked for *The Possessed* by Dostoevsky, a collection of John Cheever short stories, and a James Patterson book; my taste has always spanned fairly wide.

But it didn't matter how many plays I reenacted or books I read; I really lost it when I was in prison. My nervous system shut down to the point that if I had to spell my name, I was literally spelling it backward. And the summer of 2007 was the hottest summer I could remember so you'd better believe it was fucking hot in prison. I started to really fall apart and every second was extended torture.

The guys I was in there with were monsters, but so were the guards. Eventually I met some people who weren't as bad as the others—guys like me, who were addicts just in there for possession. But a high ratio of the people in there were extremely mentally ill. Some had been there for thirty years. And just being around people like that made you want to throw up.

When I went to the yard the first time, I took about four steps before somebody said, "Give me a piece of that Hollywood ass; I'm gonna fuck it until it gives me money." I had to fight him off. That's when I learned the way things worked there: the white guys were in a gang called the peckerwoods, unless they were Aryan Brotherhood, in which case their gang was called AB. There was also the Mexican

Mafia, the Norteños the Sureños, the Bulldogs, the Crips, the Bloods, the CCI, and a few other groups.

The peckerwoods came to my cell later and said, "Hey, mother-fucker, shave your head; you're with us now. You're going to do what we say or we're going to kill you." You don't have any choice but to pick a gang in prison. You need a gang to protect you from the prisoners and the guards. Frankly, the guards were worse than the inmates. I saw guards betting on fights and letting inmates fight each other to the death. And I had a couple of close calls with getting stabbed and they couldn't have cared less.

People have nothing to do in prison. There are no girls there and there's literally nothing to do but fight. That's what most of those guys have done their whole lives, and they're angrier than fucking hell and they're in a gang and they're doing life and they've got nothing to lose and they don't care about a goddamn thing. That's the mentality.

One day, one of the old-timers told me, "Look, Sizemore, you're going to get out of here; everyone knows you're leaving real soon. So if you're not careful, someone's going to kill or frame you because no one wants anyone going home." Because of that, in my last forty-odd days I just stayed in my cell. I didn't talk once for seventeen days. I didn't even shower. It upsets me to think about prison because prob-ably about 60 percent of the people in there are innocent, and it's the most horrible place on earth.

I worried that prison would change me in a way that it would be im-possible to come back from. I was already worrying that I had gone too far—in terms of legal trouble and drugs—before prison. But in prison I felt I had probably altered myself in not just some physiological way but also some fundamental emotional way. I felt, essentially, an entire loss of innocence. Most people don't lose their innocence all at once, but I did. I learned about a kind of loneliness I'd never experienced before. People came to visit me—my little brother Paul would come with his girlfriend and bring me Whoppers and cigarettes and other things I couldn't get, and Jinele would bring the boys. But it was almost harder when people came. One time, one of my boys saw my shackles and asked, "Why do you have those chains on you?" It was all so heartbreaking.

I was released on December 16, 2007. I had no idea what kind of life—if any—I'd have in store for me. And when I first got out, I could barely talk. I felt like I'd never been on planet Earth before. I'd only been gone nine months but it was so overwhelming that it was like all my years of life before had been erased. I didn't know how to go into 7-Eleven to buy a pack of cigarettes anymore. I was never a tough guy and never did I realize that more than when I was in prison and then got out. I'm a guy who, when it comes down to it, is afraid of the dark.

When I was first released, I wanted to talk about what I'd been through but I just couldn't. I was so ashamed. People were worried about me because I couldn't talk about it. But I was so fucking scared that I was going to end up going back. They make you think that when you leave—they say, "You'll come back, motherfucker, see you in a minute." Inmates yell that at you for weeks when they know you're leaving. I thought my personality had been forever destroyed by my experience, and in all honesty, I think some of it really was. I'd always been a curious person and I'd always been an outgoing person when I was comfortable. And the fact is, my curiosity and other aspects of my personality were quelled, if not killed, by my time away. I still haven't given up hoping that they'll come back, though.

WHILE I WAS away, in October 2007, VH1 had started airing *Shooting Sizemore,* the show that Tijuana Entertainment had made out of the footage I'd sold them, and suddenly I was dealing with the aftermath of that. I was horrified by the end result. I'd only taped what was happening so that it could be used as a sort of cautionary tale—to show people what meth can do to you.

I showed myself smoking speed on camera as a warning to children, but the way they used it made it look as if I were glorifying it. In what I gave them, I'd talk to the camera every time I smoked speed, saying things like "This stuff is ruining my life and I want you to know what I've accomplished in life—what kind of a person I was." I'd talk about everything I'd done and how meth had made those accomplishments meaningless. Then I'd say, "Why on earth would you ever do this to yourself? I don't know why I have, and the most important thing I can tell you is if you're not doing it, don't start, because you're just going to have to stop, and I can't." That's a powerful message, but the company wasn't interested in a powerful message. They didn't play the footage of me saying, "I'm not a hero, I'm a drug addict. I picked dope over family, friends, and career." They didn't show any of that. My thinking had been that if I could warn people about meth by showing what it had done to me, something positive could actually come out of my addiction. But just about the only good thing I can say about the show is that it opened the door for *Celebrity Rehab with Dr. Drew*.

I couldn't really watch *Shooting Sizemore*—I'd only watch little bits—but my mom would call me and say, "Those people are motherfuckers, Tommy," so I knew it was bad. And life wasn't all that great in general, since all I was doing was meeting up with my probation officer and getting tested. I managed to stay sober by enrolling in Matrix, an outpatient recovery program out of UCLA, and I drove out to Bakersfield for each drug test. Like I said, I was terrified of ending up back in prison again.

I have to say that my probation officer was actually a wonderful woman named Tabitha Raber; it would have been so much worse for me had she not been such a nice person. Don't get me wrong—she was tough. If you fucked up, she'd jail you. But Mrs. Raber cut me some breaks.

You have to go in for your progress report every quarter—just like in rehab. You go in there, and if anything happened, your PO writes it down. Even if you test dirty, they can arrest you, but they tend not to. And amazingly, I started using again. When I tested dirty, they ended up putting me back in treatment twice, both for ninety days. That was most of 2008 for me: using, testing, rehab.

I MET A girl named Monroe at the Seventh Veil, a strip club on Sunset. I saw her dancing and thought she had a beautiful body. It took me a little while to convince her to come home with me—about four visits—but when I convinced her, I really convinced her because she actually just moved into the apartment I'd been able to rent with the *Shooting Sizemore* money.

Monroe was a very kind person who was born into a socioeconomic background that was just horrendously impoverished and devoid of any kind of hope, in the poorest parts of Oakland. Her chances of doing anything with her life were very small.

We did some dangerous things together. Once, when we wanted drugs and didn't have any money, she introduced me to a gang member who fronted us a thousand dollars' worth of speed. I didn't know he was a gang member, but when I didn't call to pay him the next morning at ten, my phone rang at 10:05 and he left a message saying, "Hey, look, motherfucker, I'm coming over with a handgun and I'm going to shoot your fucking ass." Monroe and I left the house, and then

I actually had to call my brother Aaron and borrow the money from him.

By this point I was doing heroin with the speed and I felt like I just didn't know how to do drugs anymore. They were beyond not working; they were destroying me. At that point, I'd met with the producers of *Celebrity Rehab with Dr. Drew.* I had met Drew six years before, when I'd been trying to get sober, and my old drug dealer Bob Forrest had actually stayed sober all these years and started working with him.

I had talked to them originally about doing the first season back when I'd just gotten out of prison and was clean. Drew had predicted back then that I would relapse because I wasn't going to meetings or doing anything to stay sober—and, of course, he was right. And then I got a call when they were putting together their second season, so I went in to meet with John Irwin and Damian Sullivan, who were the producers, at the end of 2007. At that point, it was like I had one foot in the real world and one foot in the surreal subworld I was mostly operating in. I remember I had on a nice Ralph Lauren Polo shirt but my jeans were full of holes. I had a meeting with them but I sort of thought of the show as being the last stop on the block. And, amazingly, I didn't think I'd reached that point yet.

But about a year and a half later, I was desperate. Monroe and I were holed up, really high, at this house, on Kings Road above Sunset Boulevard, that a producer I know keeps for friends of his who are in trouble and need somewhere to go.

I had serious doubts by then that I would ever have an acting career again—not to mention ever get clean. I was destroyed, and I could have easily died or killed somebody while driving or been arrested again and gone back to prison for seven years. There were so many disasters that were imminent. The list of things that would have happened if I continued to use was monumental. I was definitely at the point where it was either die or go brain dead from drugs, get institutionalized, get arrested again, kill myself, or become a street person and disappear into the mist. I was out of options. So one night, I started crying and said to Monroe, "I'm going to die from this or go brain dead." And I wrote down the names Dr. Drew Pinsky, Bob Forrest, and Las Encinas Hospital. I said to her, "Get one of them on the phone and tell them it's a life-or-death situation." She called Drew the next day and he said they'd come over. But I was so fucked-up that when I knew they were coming, I snuck out the back window and left. And then the same thing happened again. She called them, and I left before they got there. I ran down to Pink Dot, a delivery supermarket place that's home base is on Sunset right near where I was staying. I'd been such a good customer for so long that the guy agreed to let me hide there in the bathroom, and when Bob came running in, asking the guy if he'd seen me, he did me a solid and said no.

But I told the show people again that I was in for sure. And I thought I was but then I got high again and didn't show up when I was supposed to. I guess the show had started—they were into the fifth day I think—and they had my name on the placard, but I wasn't there. The thing was, Monroe and I were so far gone that we were almost incapable of taking care of ourselves. I suddenly realized that we hadn't eaten in at least a day, but we were too high to figure out a way to get food. So I called the *Celebrity Rehab* production company and said, "Hey, I'm up here in this house and we don't have any food."

Two of the producers and Bob showed up and they literally threw a John's Pizza on the porch. We devoured it, but we were paranoid and high and didn't feel ready to stop what we were doing, so we didn't let them inside. The next day, it was pretty much the same situation. We were starving and didn't have food or a way to get it, so I called the production company again and they came back and threw another pizza onto the porch. They joke that they got me to commit by luring me with pizza, and it's not inaccurate. Drew was with them this time, so I let Drew and Bob inside, but I didn't want them filming anything. From there, I agreed to go in.

Of course, by the time I got there, I was having second thoughts again. But I checked in, saw Drew, and let them take blood and everything. I was so high and out of it that I kept forgetting that there was a TV show involved. When I first pulled up to go in and there were cameramen shooting what was happening, I thought they were paparazzi guys and told them to fuck off.

Celebrity Rehab had already booked Heidi Fleiss for the season—something I found out about on the way over there—and I wasn't sure how she was going to react to seeing me or, honestly, how I was going to react to seeing her. But she embraced me and when she did, it was like everything she put me through—and all of the horrible things we went through together—disappeared and we were only there to help each other get sober. Everyone was really nice, and I wanted to want to stay, but for reasons I can't quite explain, I still couldn't surrender. I told Drew and Bob that I needed to go see my kids, but I promised to come back by that night. They knew I only wanted to leave to get high, and they kept saying that if I left, I wouldn't come back.

Drew gave me a shot of Ativan to try to calm me down but it barely affected me and certainly didn't derail me. So I left with friends and I guess Drew told Will, the tech on the show, to follow me and do whatever he had to do to get me to come back. Will followed me to the house on Kings Road. He told me later that I'd accidentally left three of the burners on in the house; the entire place smelled so strongly of gas that a normal person walking in would have gotten an instantaneous migraine. I hadn't noticed a thing.

When we got there, he gave me these two pills that I guess were

300 milligrams of Seroquel each. Seroquel is an antipsychotic but it has the side effect of causing extreme fatigue. It's basically an instant sedative. Some people say it mimics a pot high; all I know is that at first I didn't feel anything, and I was still so determined to do meth that I went into my bedroom and took a gun holster I had and laid it out on the bed so that Will and the rest of the crew could see it from where they were in the house. Then I went into the bathroom, which was attached to the bedroom, and called out, "Nobody better come in here," to make them think that I actually had a gun and would shoot anyone who tried to stop me.

I just wanted one last hurrah. But once I was in the bathroom, all the Seroquel suddenly hit me, and even though I was holding a pipe, a lighter, and meth, I was suddenly so out of it that I swear to God I couldn't figure out how to get high. I don't really remember what happened after that very well, but Will told me later that I wandered out of the bedroom and said, "Man, you tell that Dr. Drew that I don't know what he gave me but he sure knows what he's doing."

I was pretty compliant at that point, so they were able to take me back to the unit and check me in. But I still hadn't surrendered entirely to the situation, and I asked Monroe to come and visit me and bring me drugs. When she showed up, though, the nurse wouldn't let her in unless she took a drug test, and she didn't want to so she couldn't see me. So she took the meth she had brought me and stashed it in the garbage can of one of the bathrooms. Naturally, they have cameras all over the place, so one of the nurses saw her do it and pulled it right out. But by then I had just passed out. I slept the sleep of someone who had been on a ten-year run and I didn't get up for a few days. And when I finally did, I wandered out to the back patio and saw that there were cigarettes and food and people I knew and liked and I figured I might as well stay.

CHAPTER 8

C☉MING T☉

I DID *CELEBRITY REHAB,* honestly, for the money.

The truth is that I'd disappointed myself so often that I simply didn't think sobriety was possible for someone like me. I was acting like I was sure that everything was going to work out, but I didn't believe it. I only behaved that way for my family and close friends because I didn't want them to worry any more than they already had, but I actually had serious doubts I'd ever get any semblance of a real life back. Ironically, if I'd actually thought I'd ever have a career again, I would never have done *Celebrity Rehab,* because I thought of it as something for also-rans and has-beens.

And yet despite the humiliation of even being on that show in the kind of shape I was in—despite many humiliating things—I was actually able to get clean.

In my first few days of being there, I was so disconsolate and hopeless and physically drained that I could only sleep. Bob told me later that he thought I was avoiding life and hiding in bed the first few days I was there, and maybe there's an element of truth in that, but I was mostly just emotionally and physically exhausted. My spirit felt like a dusty road. It had taken a lot of work to get that fucked-up. And once I started to get any kind of foothold in getting things repaired, seeing what I'd done with my life was almost too much to bear. I was heartbroken by my life—by how lost and untethered I was. I had no real agent anymore to connect me to my old life—which I considered my real life or at least the life I wanted. I'd become a pariah. I knew that people were looking at me and saying, "What a shame." I fell so far down that people either feared me or thought I was pathetic. As Dennis Rodman told me on the show, I'd gone from Hollywood to Hollyweird.

Clearly, the drugs had stopped working for me. For at least nine months before I got clean, I'd go to bed saying, "I'm not doing this stuff tomorrow, it doesn't work," but then wake up and do them. I'd sit in the bathroom and do two hundred dollars' worth of speed and heroin and leave the bathroom thinking, "I don't feel any better. I don't feel sick, but I don't feel any better." I'd have terrible stomach indigestion and be sweating and awake, not dope-sick exactly, and still wanting to reach that place drugs are supposed to let you reach, but I couldn't. When you're in that place—when you're too destroyed to continue to live with drugs but too terrified to really begin to accept the idea of living without them—death starts to seem like a welcome possibility. And when you're wishing that the drugs would kill you but they're not—well, I can't think of a worse place to be.

In retrospect, the people that I had working as my handlers were not acting in my best interest—not even close. I get the fact that, in my incapacitated state, I was a walking target; I vaguely recall even being pushed to sign legal documents without any idea of what I was signing. It's unbelievable—I somehow ended up with only about $50,000 for both *Celebrity Rehab* and *Sober House* out of the $250,000 I was paid. And I had to pay taxes on the full amount. I still haven't had the energy to go after these people who took advantage of me and whom I trusted, although maybe I will someday.

While I was aware of the fact that I was on a show, I was going through terrible withdrawal almost the entire time and didn't really wake up to everything that was happening until the show was over and I was on *Sober House*. I barely noticed the cameras on *Celebrity Rehab*. But this time, unlike all the other times I'd been in rehab, I really, really wanted sobriety. If Drew had told me that in order to achieve it, I'd have to stand on my head for five years, I would have stood on my head for five years.

Later, when I watched the show, I saw so many things that I didn't remember. Plus, I had no idea how bad I looked. Like many drug addicts, I was very skinny, but I thought back then that I looked good skinny. Instead, I just looked ill. And there was so much sadness in my eyes. When I watched some of my first couple of private sessions with Drew, I thought, "The guy sitting with Drew looks like the saddest guy who ever lived." It made me cry to look at myself. Watching it, I had another period of grieving, but I was also grateful to have that footage as evidence, because I have the propensity to forget how bad things were.

Being in rehab and shooting the show with Heidi was complicated, obviously. She was very sweet and welcoming at first. She hugged me and made me food and rubbed my hair and basically acted like she loved me. I think she was really shocked when she found out how low my drug addiction had taken me. In one of our group sessions, Bob said something about how I was a "complicated case" and Heidi snapped, "What's complicated? He's a drug addict." And Bob said that while that was indeed the case, in the face of circumstances that would have gotten most anyone else to stop—mainly prison and homelessness—I kept on going. She looked completely shocked and said to me, "You're homeless? When I left you, you were in a two-million-dollar house and making two hundred thousand dollars a week!" I nodded and I could see, despite her tough-as-nails exterior, how much that affected her.

But I think the fact that I had Monroe in my life and coming to see me made Heidi crazy. It also made me a little crazy—but in a different way. During one of Monroe's visits, just when I was starting to get into the idea of getting sober, I was suddenly overwhelmed by my desire to get high. Drew used to say that he could see me smell the joy of doing drugs—he called it the "siren of the drug"—just by seeing Monroe. That day, I started sweating like crazy and itching, almost as if being around her and remembering what it was like to get high with her actually made me high. It suddenly felt like I had no choice but to surrender to my cravings. So I told Drew I was leaving and asked Monroe to take me home. It wasn't until I got to the car that I realized—or really, remembered—what I'd be giving up if I left. I saw very clearly that I might not make it back if I got in that car. So I walked back into the unit and sat by the pool, shaking and trembling and realizing that I had just been seconds away from giving up on this new chance at life, so I had to be very sick.

Another thing that drove Heidi crazy was the relationship I had with Kari Ann Peniche, a former beauty queen who'd come onto the show after I did and who was, honestly, being difficult. But she was just a kid, and I always defended her. Because she also happened to be a very attractive kid, that made Heidi jealous. But I went out of my way to try to be appropriate with Kari Ann. One day she took off her shirt and brought out this body paint and asked me and Mike Starr to paint a bikini on her. Mike went for it and, as a red-blooded male, I wanted to jump right in as well, but I know trouble when it's lying in front of me naked.

Drew had told me that coming off meth was particularly horrific. Meth is apparently the only drug that can impair you mentally for good. With all the other drugs—crack or heroin, even—after two or three years, everything is back intact: your dopamine, your serotonin, and your short-term memory. But with meth, it's tougher. Irritability and social difficulties are common permanent effects—and honestly, I'd already had enough issues with both of those things *without* drugs. Chronic meth abusers can struggle with violent urges, insomnia, and actual psychosis like paranoia and mood disturbances for the rest of their lives.

Still, I started to get glimpses of what life could be like when I was in there. One day, we all went to Two Bunch Palms, a resort hotel in Desert Hot Springs, and I was just sitting there in the shade on this beautiful day when I realized that for the first time in a very long time, I felt content. Just normal. I turned to one of the show producers and said, "My God, is this what it's like to be a regular person? It must be nice." Everyone laughed—but I meant it.

While I was primarily convinced that I'd ruined my life, part of me didn't believe it, and that's the part of me that got me there. And I needed to hear Drew say, "Tom, you haven't ruined your life—you need to trust me on this." I needed to hear that every day from him; otherwise, I just felt like, "Fuck it." But to hear Drew's reassuring voice say, "Tom, you'll work again, you'll be happy again, and you'll be healthy again," meant everything. And every day, he'd take the time to say it.

I still need to hear it, by the way. I'll call him up now and say, "Drew, one, two, three, go!" He knows what to say. I really enjoy my relationship with Drew now. You really can't appreciate him until you're sober; when you're high, he just seems like this really good-looking space monkey or something—like he's been sent down from another planet. Did you know I've never even seen that man sweat, even when it was about 175,000 degrees in that hospital and he was in a suit and tie? Dennis Rodman would be sweating in a tank top and Drew would be cool as could be.

Drew and Bob saved my life. Before *Celebrity Rehab*, I just didn't care. I felt so crummy. The withdrawal from that drug physically wasn't that painful—it was the mental and psychological stuff. When I could see more clearly and had some more clarity about what had gone on in the previous six years of my life, I would get so depressed that I would just go, "I don't want to care about my life, because I've ruined it." I had to work to get back to the point where I would once again care. I cared about my children, but I was in such a depressed state that I thought I'd ruined all of the opportunities I could have given them. Bob would say, "You can't do this for them—you have to do this for you." It was really hard for me to do it for myself, because part of me didn't much like me anymore.

It makes me angry whenever I hear anyone say that they think what Drew was doing with *Celebrity Rehab* was exploitative. All he was ever trying to do was educate people about how addiction is a disease, and he knew that the most effective way to do that would be to use celebrities. I don't even think he made much money from the show. He also helped Monroe get sober—he literally paid for her rehab himself—and now she's going to college. She and I are still friends, but we couldn't be together once we were sober because each of us was too resentful toward the other for letting us get so fucked-up. Bob would say that he wasn't sure if Monroe was an addict—that anyone can abuse drugs, not just addicts—but he thought it was a good idea for us to be apart from each other.

I felt, in many ways, like I was cracking wide open on *Celebrity Rehab*. On the night when they played Mindy McCready's song and showed the slide show of all of us when we were younger, I started crying, and pretty soon that turned into me sobbing uncontrollably. Of course, I wasn't the only one; everyone was crying at a certain point, even the cameramen. But I was definitely crying the hardest. The combination of that song and the new feelings that being in rehab and being sober had stirred up, along with seeing photos of all of us looking so young and full of life before the drugs had gotten to us, made me unbearably sad. But it also made me grateful in a strange way, too.

Because we had all bonded so much, I was completely shocked at the graduation ceremony when Heidi suddenly busted out with the statement that I could turn any woman gay. I had just told her that I knew she was a loving person and that she should come home—meaning back to L.A.—since she'd been living for a few years out in Nevada with a bunch of birds. For her to respond in that way stung. It was obvious that she was only saying it to make me feel bad—there would be no other reason for someone to say something that cruel—and it surprised everyone else as much as it did me. We all just sat there for a minute afterward going, "Wait a minute; did that really just happen?" But Bob told me to just ignore it, and I did.

Celebrity Rehab is shot in only three weeks, but for me it was even shorter because I didn't come in until they were on day nine, and I slept for the first few days. I was, essentially, still kicking when it was over, so I chose to pay to go live in the NASH House, which is the sober-living facility on the Las Encinas grounds, for nine days before moving on to *Sober House,* the reality show that followed the recent alumni from *Celebrity Rehab* as they tried to adjust to sober life. At that point, my head was still a dirt road. And I was afraid that if I didn't stay at NASH—if I went home instead before *Sober House*—I'd just get high.

By the time I was doing *Sober House,* I'd reentered the world of the living again. I didn't have anything that real people have anymore—a bank account, a driver's license, a car, or any of the things that everyone just takes for granted. Damian Sullivan, one of the *Rehab* producers, went with me to put a lot of those things in place again. We went to the DMV in Van Nuys and got me a license, and he went with me to the bank to open an account. He also came with me to a court appearance in Bakersfield, where the judge told me that if I violated probation one more time, I'd go to prison again.

Everything with Heidi grew even more complicated at the house. Kari Ann continued to be problematic for everyone, and I kept defending her. When it got to the point where people were saying, in front of Kari Ann, that they didn't want her in the house, my heart went out to her. I went up and comforted her and told everyone to stop jumping on her. That just drove Heidi insane. When I walked down the hall with Kari, Heidi yelled after us that I was a pervert and that Kari Ann and I should both leave.

Eventually, all of Heidi's jabs got to me and I left the house. Everyone thought I was going to get high but I just wanted to cool off—so I went back to where Monroe was staying and spent the night. I tested clean and thought everything would be okay, but then Heidi kept at it until I completely snapped. I ended up going off on Mike Starr, really just because he was sitting there, and I can't tell you, especially now that he's gone, how horrible I feel about that. Heidi and I eventually made up, and some days she'd be incredibly affectionate with me, sitting on my lap and telling me how good I looked. Nobody understood our relationship and, to be honest, I was right there with them. Our relationship was so bizarre to everyone that we actually started talking about doing another reality show together for VH1, one that involved the two of us becoming roommates. I wasn't entirely serious about the idea, but I was entertaining it, although obviously it never came to fruition—which I think is definitely for the best.

But I had finally walked through that first layer of withdrawal and realized I was willing to do the footwork: to call people and make amends and look at my behavior in an honest way. I had never wanted to do that before. I'd always thought I was better than other people because I wasn't willing to do that, but really it was the other way around.

I was starting to feel like I was getting it together by the time I was doing *Sober House,* especially in comparison to some of the other people around. It was complete chaos. As Bob said back then, "When Tom Sizemore's the sanest person in the house, you know you've got a problem."

I GOT RELEASED into the real world in June 2009, and Drew had suggested I take at least six months off before I started working again. But I wanted to follow Robert Downey Jr.'s recommendation that I hire a sober coach. Robert had said that if a coach helped me to not use even just one time, he'd be worth every dollar, but I knew I'd have to start working again to be able to afford one. Of course, people weren't exactly lining up outside Las Encinas to hire me, and I was still trying to reacclimate to sober life anyway. I was also single for pretty much the first time in my life. It used to be that even when I was with someone, I had a decent idea of where I was going next. But I knew I had to be alone for a while if I was going to be able to change at all.

Honestly, early sobriety was really hard. Probably my favorite thing about drugs was that I always knew how they were going to make me feel, and I really missed that. My emotions would flare up.

I'd be looking for a pair of shoes and not be able to find them and suddenly my thoughts would go, "I probably lost this pair of shoes. Just like I lost my house. Just like I've lost everything that mattered to me." I would catastrophize everything. I'd sit in the back of Bob Forrest's truck going to meetings and sometimes I'd be thinking, "I hate you, Bob. I hate your hair, I hate your hat, I hate this truck, I hate going to this meeting in the middle of the day." Still, other days I would go and feel grateful and really proud of my sobriety. But I needed the group to hold me up and help me to be more honest about my feelings. I used to minimize everything and try to act like I was a tough guy, when really I just played tough guys in movies and behaved like one in front of the press because I thought that was what a man did. The truth is that I have always been a softy. And it felt surprisingly good to admit all of this, which is good because the pressure of being the tough guy or the cool guy or the drug guy was exhausting. People were surprised when they found out what I was really like: that I was actually a momma's boy with a master's in fine arts who loved Shakespeare.

I'd been around AA rooms since 1991, and the meetings in and around Hollywood never seemed to work for me, so I started going to AA downtown. I knew that people were gossiping about me—"I wonder if he's really getting high," that kind of thing. But after a while, that stopped. I started going to a group made up of around twenty-five people, mostly men, and I started going to meetings outside the meeting—coffee and all that. But I saw that there were people in AA who didn't blend life with sobriety—people whose only friends were their fellow sponsees. Bob told me he thought that was unhealthy—that you have to get back into normal life as much as you can. You can't be around dangerous people, but you can't only be around alcoholics in recovery, either, because that's not really living.

I started hanging out around the Midnight Mission in downtown L.A., going to the AA meeting down there and then staying and volunteering. I somehow felt comfortable there in a way that I didn't in Hollywood AA. No one down there cares about how you look or where you've been. The homeless people down there are completely forgotten about by society, and I really felt for them. And taking the focus off me and putting it on them changed my perception of things. I began to see how truly lucky I was.

Bob would tell me I had to do sobriety the way he did it and the way he helped Robert Downey Jr. and Anthony Kiedis to do it, by going to this specific meeting he's been going to for fifteen years. He'd say that going to that meeting and feeling uncomfortable would do more for me than going down to the Mission and talking to those guys. But I did it my way, and it worked. I used to think going to a meeting was a big deal—I fought it for so long—but it's an hour long and it's easy once you get in the rhythm of it. It's just like anything else in life: you can make it into a good habit in the same way that you can make doing drugs into a bad habit. And it takes a lot less time to stay clean than it does to stay high. Even just getting the dope was a full-time job.

Once I got really organized and was doing all my AA and therapy things, I would finish everything I had to by two in the afternoon, unless I was going to go to an evening meeting, and I wouldn't know what to do with myself. So I would call Drew and say, "I've done everything—went to a meeting, volunteered, and met with my sponsor—and still have nine hours before bed, so what should I do?" At one point he said, "You're going to need to get a hobby." I said, "What's a hobby?" And he said, "Tom, please." But I was serious; I really didn't know. I'd never done anything for fun, for years, besides drugs. I like to play football, or even just throw a football against a wall, but I take it so seriously that that doesn't really feel like a hobby, either. He said, "A hobby is something you don't do for any kind of money and is ideally not competitive. It's something that's all positive and fun—where you're not trying to be better than the next guy." So I said, "How about the guitar?"

Although I'd been in a band before—Day 8—I didn't play an instrument; I just sang. And it's not like I really learned how to play guitar really well or anything. I mostly just sat there like a bump on a log unless someone gave me something to play. Of course, nowadays you don't have to play an instrument to be a musician—you just have to have a six-pack and a couple of arrests and you can be inducted into the Rock and Roll Hall of Fame.

I did start to miss the band, though. My former guitar player, Rod Castro, had become a really popular session guitarist and my bass player, Tyrone Tomke, had started scoring a lot of TV shows. And it was because I kept getting arrested that the band dissolved. We had thirty-eight songs and actually produced a four-song demo that got some attention. But since that was over, it was nice to still be musical, and I enjoyed screwing around on the guitar.

I also spent a lot of time around Bob Forrest. We didn't go on fishing trips or to clubs or anything like that, either: all we did was go to meetings and bookstores and Amoeba Music, and all we'd talk about was sobriety. Drug counseling is an imperfect science, and Bob has his own style, but what's great about him is he's just so curious about everything, which makes him a good counselor. He told me once, "Tom, you have no idea why people do drugs—every week someone gives me a new reason, and it will blow my mind." I see his job mostly as someone who sees through the bullshit. He's somehow able to tell when people are lying and also when they really want to get sober, which is a great gift.

A lot of getting sober involved becoming sane for the first time in a long time, and a lot of that involved realizing that I couldn't control what other people did. I couldn't control what Heidi did, and I couldn't control what Drew wanted me to do or what my mom was thinking or what someone who interviewed me was going to write. All I could control, I saw, was my reactions to these things.

I also realized that I couldn't really control how I *felt* a lot of the time. All I could do was remind myself that things change. I used to have a false sense of security that I could control things, but I saw that I couldn't even control my own kids. I could give them a "time-out" if they did something bad, but I wasn't necessarily going to be there later to know whether they were going do whatever it was again with their mom or her parents. I could only say to the boys, "I don't approve, but I love you."

When you're using drugs and it gets bad, you blame everybody but yourself. You forget that there are decent people out there rooting for you. But suddenly I was encountering people who were walking up to me with tears in their eyes—strangers who would say, "Oh my God, you're alive. You made it. You look good!" Of course, there are a lot of mean people and horrible things that have been said, but I could finally see the great things, too. You lose sight of that when you're using drugs—you just think everybody's an asshole, everybody's against you, and the world sucks. And it's just not true.

I started to see how immature I'd been and how much I'd been coddled in my life. I saw with incredible clarity the extreme permissiveness that is given to successful actors and how, because of that, you can become a monster before you even know it. I used to think the idea of "surrendering"—as they say in the program—was garbage. I used to say that something about it didn't feel right. But I think it was more fear of doing it that made me say that. But even when I finally surrendered, it was still hard. It certainly didn't mean that the difficult times were over.

Of course, my regrets about what I should have done differently began seeping into my thoughts along with all the new recovery thoughts. I never really defended myself during those years when I was doing nothing but getting in trouble, because when I did talk, I made an ass of myself. I was falsely accused, intoxicated all the time, and being hounded, and I'd never been in that situation before so I didn't know what the protocol was. I'd learned in playing sports as a kid that if you don't know what to do, don't do anything. But I'd get high and then forget I'd decided not to do anything. I just wish I'd gotten some kind of advice about what to do, about how to address the accusations in a sane way, instead of doing what I did—which, at times, was to start mocking the police. Before all the bad stuff started happening, I always liked the police. I'd played them a lot in movies and knew them from researching roles and riding around with them. In getting clean, at least I started to repair some of those relationships.

I also started to repair my relationships with my family. My mom had stood by me the whole time, and she did her best to not make me feel any worse than I already did. She has this kind of funny thing she does where she says "delete" if you bring up something unpleasant. If I brought up prison, she'd say, "Oh, Tommy, I deleted that a long time ago. I deleted all the years you were in trouble. I don't know what happened. Ask me anything." I said, "Do you remember when I went to trial?" and she said, "Nope, delete."

In a lot of ways, I've actually been able to even forgive Heidi, even when she was saying crummy things to me on television. It was hard to hear those things, but I know she only said them because she was hurt. I'm not interested in revenge. Obviously, I wish that whole thing had never happened, but you can't reverse time. In my ideal world, she would go to the press and say "He never hit me." Then I would have true closure. But that's not going to happen.

But I realized that I had to forgive people because I still hoped to be forgiven for a lot of the things that I'd done. I shot heroin while making *Heat,* which was irresponsible. It ended up not hurting the movie, but that's just a fluke. It could have affected thousands of people—the crew, Michael Mann, the other actors—but I never thought of it that way.

In the early days of sobriety, I'd sometimes wish I were still in rehab—say, the fifth month when you're feeling great and can get up and do the daily meditation and then run five miles. I do well with a schedule, which is why movies are good for me, since you have to be somewhere at a certain time. But when I became responsible, I'd have to fight the temptation to lie in bed, knowing I had to get up for a meeting and that I wouldn't have time to work out before and I'd never work out after because it'd be too late and I'd then want to do some creative work and take a walk and throw the football. I'd be stressed before I'd gotten out of bed, and I wouldn't even technically have anything to do.

But after a while, I knew it was time to start trying to do all that I'd ever wanted to do: to act again. Robert Downey had warned me that you get in a position where you're sober and you really want everything back again, but you're worried that if you do get it back, you're only going to get fucked-up again because suddenly you once more have access to money and everything else that goes with it. But I understood that I wouldn't know unless I tried, and it was time to try.

ONE OF THE first movies that I did once I got clean again was called *White Knight.* The title was changed to *Cellmates* along the way, but when I was doing it, it was called *White Knight*. It was a comedy about the KKK, and while those things don't normally go together, the cowriter and director, Jesse Baget, is a true talent, and he was able to pull it off.

My character in that movie goes through an evolution not unlike my own. He transitions from being this very shut-down, hateful, racist southern man to a sort of 1967 Summer of Love hippie who falls in love—and it's all funny, if you can believe it. There's a part when one of the characters hands my character a note that says, "Anybody can change, but only if they really, really want to," and when I first read the script, I just started crying, because it's so true. It made me realize that we all get second chances—some people, like me, even get nineteen chances.

The opportunity came along at the right time, because I really thought I'd ruined my career and was actually thinking about trying to work as a drug counselor. Bob had said he thought I could have a future in it. I honestly didn't know what else I could do since I didn't have many traditionally marketable skills or interests. All I've ever really liked to do is read, see movies, look at art, and be around people, which doesn't exactly make you very viable in the working world.

The script was 116 pages of pure dialogue, and I was in every single scene. The first reading didn't go very well because I was nervous, so then Jesse and I spent about four solid days together, just talking about the script and watching movies like *Raising Arizona* and *Oh Brother, Where Art Thou?* to try to get into the tone of the movie. It can sometimes take me a little while to warm up to doing the work, which gave us time to just sort of hang out and bond. We'd toss a football back and forth on the roof and keep talking.

We shot for thirteen days in downtown L.A. The way I work is I learn my dialogue but then wait to really perform it when the director says "Action." So I don't really have a chance to see how it works until the first take. Because of that I stumbled a bit on the first takes, but then would nail it on the second.

The movie walks a fine line and I was a little scared that I was going too big with the character. I'd ask Jesse, "Are you sure we're not going a little too broad with this?" He'd say, "No, trust me"—so I did. Being funny in a movie is hard. Timing and delivery is everything. You also need to be with other people who are funny, and Jesse created the right atmosphere for that.

Jesse told me that I added a lot more emotion to the role than he'd expected me to—that in my first speech about all the hardships I'd suffered as a Klan member, I grounded the character so much that you actually feel for the guy, rather than just hearing a speech that was actually intended to be funny and sort of facetious.

Because I was so focused and trying so hard to prove myself, I wasn't getting a lot of sleep over those two weeks, and I actually fell asleep when we were shooting these scenes of me lying down in jail. But I'd just wake up and keep going. One of the amazing realizations I had while doing that movie was that I was facile again—meaning that if I thought a scene should go a certain way and it started to go another way, I'd be able to transition with ease. I was very rigid with my acting when I was using because I just wanted to get through the scenes, and I used to have this attitude when acting of "If it's a square peg, I'm going to fit it in this round hole—I'll make it work, goddamn it."

When I could afford to, I hired a sober companion—this Nazi-type guy with long hair who would say things like "You've got to do what I tell you to do—I'm not here to play." He wasn't a lot of fun but he was still a very nice man. And people started to get less worried about hiring me. I'd have a physical before a shoot and have my blood taken, which would show I was clean. You can fake a lot of things but you can't fake blood.

I knew that the long-term plan was to work as much as possible but that I'd have to start small. I also knew that the end goal was to get full-time custody of my kids and then be able to give them whatever they needed to succeed in life and send them to college. But at this point I still just owed money.

While I couldn't believe people were willing to give me another chance, at the same time I know that America loves to watch people rise and fall and rise again. For some reason, it's built into our culture and DNA to enjoy seeing people from the highest heights fall the greatest distances and then watch those very same people dig themselves out of the mire and re-ascend to that hallowed place. I think that unconsciously people are jealous of success, so the fall is somewhat satisfying. But then I think they like to see the rise again because it sort of affirms for them that anything's possible—and in turn makes them feel better about their own struggles.

Still, there are a lot of actors who have fallen and never come back. People like Brad Renfro, who was never a big star but probably would have been had he not struggled with addiction—and also probably could have gotten his life and career completely back on track had he not died of a drug overdose. And Chris Farley. So many others. When Downey made it all the way back, I thought, "I'm happy for him, but how many of us can there be?"

I was about to find out.

CHAPTER 9

TODAY

IT'S AMAZING WHAT you learn about yourself when you stop doing drugs. It's amazing what I've learned. In sobriety, I started to do things I never would have thought I'd ever be interested in. I started to draw and do Photoshop stuff and teach my boys how to ride dirt bikes. I joined an intramural flag football league—something I would never have done as an active addict and probably wouldn't have done if I hadn't gone through what I've gone through. I also tried to reacquaint myself with the things I really enjoy doing. Like my dad, I'd always been a big reader, but during those last few years of using, I'd stopped even doing that. Now I picked up books again. And I got back into exercising—almost obsessively for a while by doing it twice a day. Drew and Bob had drilled it into my head that one of the key things for me would be to eliminate free time and to fill it productively.

Once I got some clarity about my situation, I could see that I was an addict, of course, but also that addiction is a disease and that I had a genetic predisposition to it. For a long time, I didn't know I had it—or, more accurately, I was in denial about the fact that I had it. But Bob pointed out to me all the indicators, such as all the obsessive-compulsive tendencies I can have about things and the fixation I've always had about being good at something. Even the hyperfocus I've always had on acting—which has been a good thing in many ways, because it's part of what's made me successful—isn't always healthy. I hyperfocus on football, even if it's just throwing a football against a certain spot on a parking lot wall. These sorts of obsessions are touchstones for addiction: if you have that kind of brain, you already are a potential addict. It all started to make sense. Aaron has struggled with various levels of substance abuse. My grandfather Sizemore was an alcoholic—though he stopped drinking at the age of fifty-two—and my entire family has been rife with addiction. I also saw that I had a predisposition to depression, which is also in my family. Before, when I would be in those deep, dark holes, it didn't matter if people told me, "You're talented" or "You're a good person." But in sobriety, I learned how to understand that when I was in a hole I should just ride it out—that as much as depression comes over me for no clear reason, it lifts in much the same way. Once I began to understand all of that, I was able to enjoy being me and to start to forgive myself. It was hard to do but at the same time easier than I thought it would be.

I began to focus on what sober people call "getting right-sized" and tried to train my brain to just stay clean and be a productive employee. I would talk to Downey about the attitude I really wanted to develop: the part of me that could stop thinking about myself and just be a productive part of the machine—the part that could be a good employee and a good dad. And of course, good employees and good dads don't do dope.

· · ·

WORKING TODAY IS an interesting experience. I can't tell you the number of people I encounter who say, "I thought you were dead! Where have you been?" They're often suspicious—I suppose for good reasons—and there's very much a feeling of "Let's watch him and see if he's still doing drugs" or "Let's see how much drugs have affected him" or even "Let's just watch him in general since he hasn't pitched in eight years." In sports terminology, they're watching my performance and pitch count really closely when they're giving me a starting position because they want to be sure they've made the right decision. They know that if they haven't, they need to change things when there's still a tenable alternative. I had a director I worked with recently say to me, "I know you're clean, but what's the residual impact of those drugs?" I immediately became paranoid that I was doing something to make him think I wasn't all there. Then I remembered that people have every right to be suspect. Besides, I'm fifty now and I feel my age. I don't feel good all the time and I can't do what I used to do physically. I woke up recently and thought, "Oh my God, I'm tired—getting out of this bed is hard." And look, I get it that if I'm lucky, I'll only be around thirty or thirty-five more years. I want to make the most of it.

Lately I feel like I've been doing just that—making the most of it. I'd been sort of trudging along, doing smaller sort of B movies, when Antoine Fuqua, a very big-time, talented director who did *Training Day,* called me in early 2010 about a Fox television pilot with Ethan Hawke that he was putting together called *Exit Strategy*. It was a much coveted and talked-about pilot, and he was completely straight with me: he said that when he brought my name up with the producers, it didn't exactly set the room on fire.

He came up with this strategy that I didn't think would work but it was basically to run the clock. He told me they were talking about offering the role of Ethan Hawke's mentor to people like Kevin Kline,

Stanley Tucci, and Chris Cooper, but that everyone they wanted either passed or there was always a dissenting voice in the room and the deal was that everyone had to agree. And by the Thursday before the Tuesday they were going to start, they still hadn't found someone for the role. So Antoine, completely acting, says, "Oh my God, I can't believe it, how could we have forgotten Tom Sizemore?" Apparently there was total silence in the room—this was literally the week that Charlie Sheen was going around and acting crazy when he was getting fired from *Two and a Half Men*. And no one was more against the idea than Heather Kadin, this very proper and smart executive. She apparently said something like "Wow, what a brilliant idea. Who else is coming out of rehab or prison this week that we could throw into our Ethan Hawke pilot?" But the rest of the room was open to the idea—or at least willing to be open to the idea. And finally Heather said something like "Aw, screw it, why not?"

Antoine called me and said, "Brother, sit down. You've got to come in here tomorrow. And you have to give your best work. *Private Ryan* ain't shit compared to what you have to do tomorrow—you have to blow the roof off." He got the pages over to me and told me that my audition was at Fox at 4:15 the next afternoon. I was so panicked that I couldn't even prepare for it—all I could do was worry that I couldn't do it. I'd just stare at the script and think, "I can't do it, I can't do it, I can't do it." I couldn't even remember what the hell I'd done before, back in the day when I went in for big auditions all the time.

Then, finally, I remembered. I would just read the script a lot without even trying to commit it to memory, then I'd have someone go over it with me in the morning. And just having read it a lot the day and night before would make me able to remember everything. I wouldn't put anything on it—no juice, no emotion—because I didn't ever want to do that until I was in front of the camera for the first time.

De Niro is similar. He doesn't even say the lines until he's on camera for the first time. He'll practice by saying, literally, "Blah blah blah." You run a line with him and he responds, "Blah blah blah." If you're truly a great actor, the only part that counts is "action" and "cut." The rehearsals don't count. In the NFL, they call a guy who plays real well in practice but folds under the pressure of the game a "practice player." I don't want to be a practice player in life, period, and particularly not in the performing arts.

After reading the script over and over again, I went to the roof of my building and took some notes on it, then tested myself to see if I could write down my first speech. I told myself that if I could write down six sentences perfectly, I could go to sleep. And I did. I didn't know if I had everything memorized, but it felt great.

The next morning, I read the cue lines and then my own lines into Windows Movie Maker, put it on my iPod, and listened to it. I took a steam and then had a friend run lines with me. When I did it perfectly, I decided I wasn't going to practice anymore.

I was still so goddamned nervous—so nervous that, on the way to the audition, I had to have my manager pull over so I could throw up. And driving onto the studio lot made me uncomfortable because I hadn't been on one in a long time, and I remembered that I used to be on them all the time. Then I just sort of said to myself, "The only way you're going to be on this lot regularly again is if you go upstairs and throw a touchdown pass."

When we walked into the audition room and I saw that there were around seventeen people there, I was initially intimidated, but I just tried to take control of the situation. I said, "I'd rather talk after I read. Who am I reading with?" Someone said, "Me," and I said, "Thank you. Are you any good?"

And so I went for it—and man, did it feel good. During the last few lines my character gets up and leaves, so I got up and left the room. From outside, I heard applause, and I was so happy I wanted to cry. But my manager came out and got me. "You've got to do it again," he said. "They think you were maybe lucky." And I came back and did it again and it went even better. Heather told me later that I simply blew the doors off of anyone else they had had read.

After I left, they had a real dilemma on their hands. I found out later that they'd basically said, "Well, he's the best but can we even insure him? Isn't there anyone else we can think of?" But there wasn't anyone they could come up with. Even when they'd agreed, though, they still had to get it approved by the network. At one in the morning, Antoine called me and said, "It's official. Les Moonves signed off on it." I just started weeping, I was so grateful.

We did the table read two days later and I guess the producers were so happy with how I did that they went from thinking, "Let's have this guy do as little as possible because we're not sure how reliable he is" to "Can we get the writers to write more of Tom's actual voice into his character?" and "Can we get more scenes with Tom's character in the script?"

The shoot went incredibly well. It was almost three weeks of night shoots, and I was as prepared for them as I've ever been for anything. Heather told me that I was actually the only actor who knew all his lines every day. But I was very excited to be getting another chance, and the way she treated me really helped. One day on the set, when I was just standing around, she gestured to the seat next to her and said, "Come and sit down next to me." It was a small moment, but at the same time it was huge because I felt like she was inviting me into her inner circle, and it had been a long time since I'd been invited into any inner circles I wanted to be in.

During breaks, one of the writers—David Guggenheim—and I

would discuss politics or we'd just shoot the shit. Because Heather was a nice Jewish girl, I'd jokingly break into the Jewish prayers I'd learned when I'd toyed with the idea of converting. Heather would howl. She also thought it was funny that I would wear biker jackets and biker boots when in fact I'm really this sensitive bookworm of a guy.

I guess all the producers were surprised that I was so open, because they'd been worried about how they were going to be able to talk to me about everything I'd been through. But I just told them the stories—whatever they wanted to hear, whether it was about the drugs or what happened with Heidi or the Whizzinator. At one point I remember acting out the whole Whizzinator incident for them and thinking, "How could I have gotten any of this back?"

Everyone was surprised when the show wasn't picked up and I was so shocked that I went into one of my twenty-four-hour mourning periods. There were initially plans to retool the whole thing but then Ethan Hawke pulled out and it got shelved. Still, I made what I hope will be lifelong friends with some of the people involved. Heather went from not wanting me in their office building to being one of my biggest advocates. She would tell me that I was "a walking, talking example" of why you shouldn't believe anything you read.

Once Heather got the news that *Exit Strategy* was definitely not going to happen, she asked Peter Lenkov, the director of *Hawaii Five-0*, if he'd consider writing a part for me into that show. *Hawaii Five-0*, which was a remake of the original, was a huge hit for CBS and also produced by K/O, the company that made *Exit Strategy*. Peter liked the idea so Heather set up a meeting for the three of us. I guess she had told him ahead of time that I was going to be really quiet and reserved, because that's how I'd been when I came in for my *Exit Strategy* audition. But I was in a pretty exuberant mood the day of the meeting and Peter and I really hit it off. Peter had a football in his office and we started talking about how I used to play and even tossed the ball back and forth. I was doing my Robert De Niro impressions and telling stories about shooting *Heat* and I guess Peter was looking at Heather going, "Where's the quiet guy you'd told me we'd be meeting?" But while we had fun together, the main thing I wanted to do was show him how serious I was about acting again and how hard I would work. He seemed to understand that, and once they got the idea of me appearing on the show approved by CBS, Peter had me written into an episode as a character they'd created for me: Captain Vince Fryer, the head of Internal Affairs.

When I got to Hawaii to shoot the first episode, I became suddenly very emotional just being on the set of a TV show; seeing the entire crew and this cast of people working together stirred up all of these feelings in me about what I'd lost. I guess Peter wasn't expecting me to be so emotional; he called up Heather and said, "Tom's sort of freaking out. I hope this is going to work." But I shook it off and everything went really well—so well that even though I'd been hired for one episode and that episode had complete closure, they figured out a way to write me into another five.

The more episodes I was on, the more Alex O'Loughlin and Scott Caan, the two stars of the show, started pushing Peter to make me a series regular. And though I'm told he very seriously entertained the idea, it would have basically been impossible to continue to come up with reasons to justify having a series regular who wasn't a part of the *Five-0* team. Honestly, I was happy to be involved at all.

Apparently the joke around the K/O office is that they now have to find a role for me in everything they do. As soon as they put something into development, I guess everyone says to Heather, "But who's Tom Sizemore going to play?"

I loved everything about the shoot. It was great to connect with Scott Caan, since I'd known his dad, James Caan, a long time—but probably the best part about it was that when they were putting together the episode where my character was getting killed off, they needed someone to play my wife. I suggested Maeve. We hadn't been in touch in a long time but I knew she'd continued to act and had actually moved into producing shows. I was, of course, thrilled when she agreed to sign on and even more thrilled when she came to Hawaii for the shoot. While we didn't have any scenes together, I finally got to sit down with her for the first time in a decade. I'm not going to lie; a large part of me fantasized that now that I was getting a career going again, I could win her back. But I also understood that this was, on a certain level, a fantasy. And just to be around her and have her say that she supported me and that she could see that I was in a good place meant more than I can ever express.

BECAUSE OF EVERYTHING I've been through, I definitely psych myself out when it comes to work in ways I didn't before. If you were to sit down and think about the pressure of each take—the amount of money being spent on a very large production—you wouldn't be able to work. Most actors know all this intuitively, so they don't focus on it. If you actually sat there and thought, "If you don't know your lines or if you make a mistake, you could, in effect, cost somebody a hundred and twelve thousand dollars," you'd lose your mind. But suddenly I was thinking about those things.

And honestly, the hardest part about acting, for me, is that you're sitting there on a set for fourteen hours only to act for maybe around twenty-eight minutes. So for thirteen hours and thirty-two minutes you're sitting in your trailer, and when you have a mind like mine, that's a very long time to think about a lot of bizarre shit.

But once I started to realize that things were actually going well, the more positive I felt during my downtime. I still have really bad days where I don't even believe that what's going on is going on. And then I have really good ones. When I watched one of my *Hawaii Five-0* episodes, I actually sat there and thought, "Wow, I look good—I look like a real movie star again. And I still know how to make bold choices." Of course, you can't make bold acting choices all the time but I still know how to do stuff that makes people go, "I'm willing to continue to watch this guy even if he's talking about banal shit, like the weather."

Still, sometimes I feel like I'll never escape my past. In September of 2011, when a friend who was staying with me was arrested for erratic driving, the cops came to my place to get him and arrested me as well—claiming that I hadn't finished my community service even though I'd finished it in April and had actually done extra hours. It was all because of some clerical mistake, which I told the police, but they just didn't care. Because I had just started shooting *Hawaii Five-0* and I knew this wasn't the kind of thing I needed at all, I pleaded with them, saying, "All you have to do is press a button and you can see the truth—I know it's something you can do. And if you arrest me again, I might get fired from my job." They didn't care and I didn't expect them to. Yet it was my first time getting arrested sober and let me tell you, the experience was very different; my fear level was markedly lower because I had nothing to hide. But then, of course, the press got ahold of the information and the headlines read TOM SIZEMORE ARRESTED AT DRUG HOUSE. The truth is that I was arrested at home, I was only in custody for about two hours, and when they found out that I was telling the truth, they couldn't have gotten me out of that jail fast enough.

Then, about two months later, a girl I'd been seeing, Megan Wren, was reported missing. She lived in my building and even though I consider myself pretty savvy about these things, I didn't know she was a heroin addict, because she was very smooth and clever about hiding it. Once I realized she had a drug problem, I tried to get Bob Forrest to come talk to her and also tried to help get her into different rehabs. She didn't go or clean up and her father had filed a missing persons report when he hadn't heard from her, after which somebody told him she'd been spending time with me. TMZ found out and published a story that said my girlfriend was missing and I was wanted for questioning. I hadn't heard from her for a couple days, but I got ahold of her. She had no idea what was going on but as soon as she heard that she'd been reported missing, she walked right into a police station and the whole thing was cleared up. Still, the headline remained. A good thing came out of it, though, in that the scandal totally woke Megan up and she went to rehab.

All I can do is remain positive and healthy and consistent. My son Jagger will say to me, "Dad, are you going to stay this time? Are you going anywhere?" I feel sad that I've made them nervous and created this anxiety, but it makes sense. It's a result of all those times I'd say, "I'll be right back, I'm going to the store," for instance, and not come back because I'd gotten high. More than anything, I don't want to hurt these kids. They're entirely innocent and didn't ask for any of this bullshit.

Most of my time these days, honestly, is spent working, and when I'm not working, I'm trying to relax. My life isn't really all that exciting. I take a bath every night. When I was growing up, we only had a bathtub, until we were able to jerry-rig a showerhead to it and make it into a shower, so I've somewhat always equated baths with being poor. But when I was married to Maeve, she took a lot of baths, and

I would see her in there, luxuriating with all of her salts and bubbles, and think how nice it looked. Now I do that myself.

But the focus, really, is on work. Even though I know it's not possible, I want to make up for lost time. So I played a government operative in a Bernie Madoff movie, *Madoff: Made Off with America,* which was ironic in that I think I was just about the only actor he didn't steal from—I didn't have any money to steal when he was in his prime, and besides, I was a bit caught up in my own pyramid scheme with myself.

I did a movie called *An Evening with Donald Klemsky,* where I played a blind man, and another called *El Bosc,* in Barcelona with Oscar Aibar, who's a very big deal in Spain. He's Pedro Almodóvar's protégé, and his movies are a sort of amalgamation of comedy and sci-fi. I also shot a movie called *Company of Heroes* in Bulgaria with the football player Vinnie Jones. It was based on a computer strategy game and follows a group of soldiers during World War II. I made an independent movie called *Five Hour Friends,* where I played a golfing ad executive who's fairly committed to ephemeral relationships, until he meets an outspoken attorney. And I shot a horror movie called *Slumber Party Slaughter,* which was made by the grandniece of silent movie actor Lon Chaney. I play an actor with a substance abuse problem, and while I'm not exactly sympathetic, you can see that I'm a good guy. This was definitely a case of life imitating art. The writer-director, Rebekah Chaney, actually wrote the part for me while watching me on *Celebrity Rehab.*

The work is coming and it's coming fast—just like it did in the beginning of my career. They may not all be my dream movies but I get that I'm rebuilding what I lost and that it doesn't all materialize perfectly and in an instant. That's probably for the best. A slow build means that if I do eventually get everything back, I'll be able to understand and appreciate how much it's worth.

. . .

SOMETIMES, OF COURSE, I miss the drugs. I miss feeling immune to the suffering of growing older. But at the same time, that's life, man: you're born alone, you die alone. When you're going to go, you want to look back and say, "I did something: I traveled, I met people, I was a citizen of the world, I showed kindness, I found a vocation, I became a certain person," and you're not going to be able to do that if you're on drugs. Even if you had all that before you started doing drugs, like I did, you won't be able to keep it. You've got to stop. Robert Downey Jr. stopped. River Phoenix, Brad Renfro—those guys didn't stop and they're not here anymore. When River died, out there on Sunset and Larrabee, asking for his brother—well, it just broke my heart. It broke all of our hearts. Before that, I felt invulnerable. I was becoming a star. But I was forever changed when River died. We all were. But of course, it didn't stop us from continuing the downward trajectory.

Now that I've been sober a little while, I can see my life coming full circle. I recently finished playing a wiseguy in the sequel to *Raging Bull,* and the script was written by a guy I've known for fifteen years, Rustam Branaman. We'd met back when I did *Devil in a Blue Dress* and had seen each other over the years, because he was friends with Downey and a few other people I also knew.

Once, when I was deeply into the meth but still had my Benedict Canyon house, Rustam and I started talking about De Niro and I doing a movie that Rustam would write and direct. I was pretty far gone at that point and one night, when I was really high, I videotaped myself working out on a Precor machine and talking to Rustam—basically giving him ideas for the meeting. Because I was high and somewhat confused, my notes and ideas were sort of about the movie and sort of about me, and then I went off for an hour or so about how he should actually make the movie the story of my life. I called Rustam and asked him to come over, telling him I had something for him to watch. I think I made it sound like it was a ten-minute tape or something. So Rustam came by and I put the video in. He watched it for about twenty minutes and saw I was clearly gakked out of my mind. "All right, I think I get what you're going for," he said as he started to get up to go. But I wouldn't let him leave. In my delusional state, I thought he had to see the entire three-hour tape so that he could see how brilliant my ideas were. He kept saying, "Tom, I've got to go," but I would jump up and say, "No, it'll be over any minute now—just watch this one part!" Then, if at any point I thought he wasn't paying perfect attention, I'd stop the tape and quiz him on what he'd just watched. He was such a good sport about it; he'd been sober a long time and he just listened to me run my mouth and watched the tape until I got tired. Then he said, "I think maybe you should get some sleep," and left. The next day, Jessie, who was living with me at the time, said, "I'm not sure it was such a good idea to show him that whole tape." I thought she was crazy and told her so.

A few years later, in the summer of 2004, I was driving with Jessie down Santa Monica Boulevard toward Bundy Drive and I suddenly couldn't find my meth pipe. I was on my way to get drug-tested because I was on probation, but I was so addicted at that point that I needed to get high and then figure out a way to pass the test. I went into this full-blown panic just as we were reaching Bundy, and then I remembered that there was some sort of a head shop around there, which would solve my two problems in one fell swoop: I could get a pipe and also buy synthetic urine so I could pass the test. So I stopped the car and started running around looking for this head shop. Finally I saw it and I went running in there, telling them that I needed a pipe and synthetic urine. They handed me the pipe and I asked to use their bathroom so I could go smoke some meth; the guy who worked there just gave me this look that said, "You've got to be kidding me." I was standing there holding the pipe, sweating profusely because it was the height of summer, about to go smoke meth, when who should walk in but a fresh-faced-looking Rustam. He happened to have an office above the head shop because the rent was cheap.

Then, a couple years after that, I called up Downey and lied and told him that I was sober because I knew it was the only way he would see me. It was when I was really circling the bottom of the drain—when I didn't have anywhere to live, a car, or a penny to my name. Robert and I hung out for a few minutes before he saw that I was high, and I guess he realized that he was too new at being sober to be around me in that state. So he called up Rustam and said, "Can I hand Tom off to you? Maybe you can say something that will motivate him to get sober." So Rustam came and met us at Mulberry Street Pizza in Beverly Hills. I was too high to eat, but I knew I could get some money off Rustam, so I asked him if I could borrow twenty bucks. He gave it to me and I thanked him by excusing myself to go to the bathroom and then climbing out the bathroom window. I was paranoid from how much speed I was doing and got it in my head that maybe Rustam was some super-sober guy who would chase me down, so I started running. I ended up at a nearby gas station because I knew a guy who sold meth there; once I bought the drugs, I called up the sober-living house where I was living and essentially forced the guy who answered the phone there to come pick me up and take me to a dope house.

But it's funny how life works. I got cast in the *Raging Bull* sequel and when I saw the script, there was Rustam's name on it. I hadn't seen Rustam in eight years—since I took the twenty bucks from him and snuck out the pizza parlor bathroom window. When I got to the set for the first time, I went around asking everyone where he was. An assistant went and got him. When Rustam saw me he just looked me in the eyes, saw that they were clear, and said, "So, it's really true—you really are sober." Here was a guy who had all but begged me to get sober in the past, and he was looking at me and seeing that, against all odds, I had actually changed.

Jake LaMotta was on the set that day too. It was his ninetieth birthday and the crew had arranged to have a girl jump out of a cake as a surprise for him. Now, I had become pretty fascinated with La-Motta because I'd been so fascinated with De Niro after seeing *Raging Bull,* and because I'm always going to admire a tough guy. LaMotta's still tough, even at ninety. And maybe it's because inside I'll always be a poor kid from Detroit who may act hard at times but inside is scared of the dark, but LaMotta inspires the hell out of me. Through a combination of genes, coincidence, ambition, and a hell of a lot of luck, I have finally—like LaMotta—come to see what being tough actually means. So I can't tell you what it meant to me when Jake went out of his way to find me on the set so he could say, "You look great, Tom. Just keep doing what you're doing."

I told him what I'm going to tell you: that's the plan.

ACKNOWLEDGMENTS

I'D LIKE TO ACKNOWLEDGE the following people: Anna David, Aaron Sizemore, David Vigliano, Charles Lago, Maeve Quinlan, Beth Holden, Bob Forrest, the staff at 1010 Wilshire Boulevard, Antoine Fuqua, Judy Sizemore, Heather Kaden, and Sarah Durand.

—*Tom Sizemore*

Thanks, first and foremost, are due to Tom Sizemore for trusting me with the task of sharing his life with the world. Thanks as well to Sarah Durand, who taught me how truly supportive an editor can be, and David Vigliano. I am deeply indebted to Aaron Sizemore, Damian Sullivan, William Smith, Heather Kadin, and Beth Holden for helping me to round out the story. Thanks as well to Hugh Gaspar, Thomas Edward Sizemore, Sr., Scott Silver, Peter Bogdanovich, Bob Forrest, Chris Steffen, Jessie Tuite, Jesse Baget, Rustam Branaman, and Peter Lenkov.

—*Anna David*